Glorious Rubber Stamping

Glorious Rubber Stamping

IDEAS, TIPS & TECHNIQUES

Judy Ritchie, Jamie Kilmartin, and Leslie Conron Carola

HUGH LAUTER LEVIN ASSOCIATES, INC.

Concept and development: Leslie Conron Carola, Arena Books Associates, LLC.
Design: Kathleen Herlihy-Paoli, Inkstone Design, Inc.

Projects are credited to designers on page.
Projects without credit have been created by Judy Ritchie or Jamie Kilmartin.

Book Club Edition
Printed in the U.S.

Acknowledgments
Thank you to the participants—individual designers, artists, crafters, and manufacturers— in the U.S.
and Canada— for their generous contributions to this project: Patti Behan; Dave Brethauer, Kayce
Carey; Maria Carola; Laurie Goodson; Adrienne Kennedy from My Sentiments Exactly!; Nathalie
Métivier, Marie-France Perron, and Marie Eve Trudeau from Magenta Rubber Stamps; Cindi Nelson
and Lara Zazzi from Savvy Stamps; Alexis Seabrook; Kim Smith and Stacey Turechek from The Great
American Stamp Store; Christine Timmons, Trish Turay, Jan Williams, Donna Volovski.

Jacket image credits: Top left: Alexis Seabrook; Top middle: Kim Smith; Top right: Kim Smith.
Middle left: Alexis Seabrook; Middle right: Marie-France Perron. Bottom left: Alexis Seabrook;
Bottom middle: Christine Timmons; Bottom right: Marie-Eve Trudeau.
Page 2: Christine Timmons; Page 3:Laurie Goodson; Page 5: from the top: Dave Brethauer, Hero
Arts, Dave Brethauer, Kim Smith, Kim Smith.

CONTENTS

INTRODUCTION

Have you seen what rubber stampers are creating now? Rubber stamping has grown, and some of the projects being created are phenomenal. But you don't have to be an artist to create glorious rubber-stamped projects for your friends and family. You don't need a year's supply of cardstock and paper, rubber stamps, inks, or "embellishments," either. You need *you*, *some* cardstock and papers, a *few* rubber stamps, a *little* ink, and maybe a *handful* of embellishments—ribbons, eyelets, brads, and so on. With just these few tools plus a little imagination and a few basic techniques you can create a varied array of effects and one-of-a-kind creative designs. Stamping is fun; enjoy what you are doing.

When you make cards and gifts for others you are sharing a part of yourself with them. Crafting is about celebrating life—the past, the present, and the future. We are using skills handed down to us by our mothers and grandmothers, and we are even adapting those skills and techniques to new technology. We are making connections, discovering ways we are connected to the past—the people, places, and things around us.

▲ *Flower and bee images float freely on an ivory panel mounted first on a green cardstock mat and then slightly off-center onto a split base of solid red and green with white horizontal stripes. The horizontal stripes pull your eye immediately in to the featured panel. The palette is pleasing and consistent. The bees are highlighted with the addition of a clear dimensional lacquer on the wings and with glitter on the yellow body stripes. Card by Dave Brethauer.*

◀ *A single stamp with a single color highlighted in white provides dramatic results. A classic centered image stamped in black on a metallic cardstock is enhanced with white ink, layered on to a black mat and then a white one before being centered on a rich brown card. Elegant brown-and-white silk cord knots in the four corners of the black mat add dimension. A classic, centered, stunning card.*

▶ *The weight of the small, solid color bird (bringing a tiny punched flower to the tree) in the lower left portion of this card by Kim Smith balances the tree with its lighter-colored flowers. The pearlescent paint on the tree flowers adds an unworldly lightness. The layering of the white mat on peach mats picked up from the colors of the flowers creates a perfect setting for the scene.*

Handmade cards, scrapbooks, gifts, and gift-wrapping allow real-life glimpses into your own life—who you are and what is important to you. You are creating memories for others. We seem to have lost the art of letter writing in our hectic days, but you can reach out to someone with a handmade card and brighten their day. Or why not create a special label to attach to a box of cookies, or a jar of potpourri or homemade chocolate treats you have made for someone special? I remember my mother making jars of her homemade jam. She was not an artist, but she always insisted on adding a little hand-decorated label to the jars she brought to friends or family. Years later I found many of the simple jars in my grandmother's house, well-washed but with labels intact. She had kept those jars for years, never wanting to let go of the memories they contained.

There are no hard-and-fast rules to which you must subscribe before producing an "acceptable" rubber-stamped work. Learn a few basics about well-balanced design and color, and familiarize yourself with various papers and inks and you are on your way to creating your own remarkable works of art. We always suggest, when you are starting out, that you plan your layout on scrap paper first. One trick that we teach in a basic stamping class is to divide the space in thirds horizontally and vertically (make a tic-tac-toe board). And then move the stamp images around within the sections. The most interesting visual points are near the intersecting lines, so arrange your design around one or more of these focal points, filling in the background as needed. Space is as important a design element as any rubber stamp image. Please don't feel compelled to fill up the white space on your card or project.

Gathering some fundamentals of design, balance, and color before setting out to create your own rubber-stamped projects allows your creative intuition to develop. When a project that you see in a book or magazine, or a store grabs your attention, take the time to figure out why it appeals to you. Is it the color, the size, the balance or arrangement of materials, the materials themselves, the message? Do you prefer warm (red, orange, yellow) colors or cool (blue, green, purple) colors? Are you a traditionalist? Or do you like to take chances with unusual combinations?

You will find that many of the projects in *Glorious Rubber Stamping* could be in almost any other chapter than the one in which we have placed them. Our chapters cover the gamut from simple to unexpected, sophisticated projects. Many projects were created using more than one technique, and could therefore be included in another chapter. We are offering ideas and techniques—more than 150 projects with the intention of flooding your vision with lots of ideas to keep you thinking creatively. You will find that it is easy to adapt a technique or a format to many different colors, or different kinds of projects. We had fun exploring the uses for a wonderful paper quilt that Judy made as a possible cover for the book. It didn't work out for the cover, but she made a journal for her granddaughter with the paper quilt on the cover, a scrapbook page with the paper quilt as the mat, and a charming little gift card with a few squares of the paper quilt. The designer made an album cover with the paper quilt. We hadn't planned this. It just happened. The quilt inspired lots of ideas. Let your projects do the same. Start thinking of ways to use and reuse your stamps and materials. Learn to see beyond the whole shape to its individual elements.

How do you start? Simple. Jump in and make a card for someone you really love—your sister, your mother, your spouse, your daughter or son, niece or nephew, best friend. Do something from your heart. A handmade card or gift will brighten the day of anyone you love.

▲ *A large square card by Alexis Seabrook is stamped in monochromatic rust on ivory. The frames of the stamped images are cut apart and layered together. A classic, formal composition with an elegant simple vine stamp and a beautifully-written "Thank you" at center. Look what a sense of design does.*

▶ *The blue sea beckoning from the top right echoes the column of blue sailboats at left. An interesting mixture of geometric shapes and a pleasing pallet.*

DESIGN BASICS

🐝

There are a few things to think about before starting on a project: What is the project for? Who
or what are you celebrating? What is the emotional
response to the event—for the recipient and for you?
Should the project be large or small? What color
scheme would be appropriate—yours or the recipient's? Do you and the recipient share the same taste in
color and basic design? Do you know the recipient's
favorite colors? Will you use some decorative accents?
Jot down your responses to these questions and use the
answers as a checklist to consult as you make the project. Nothing is dictated, but most rubber-stamping
projects rely on good composition, pleasing rhythm,
and harmonious color. Trust your own eye to tell you
what works and what doesn't work. Do you like the
way the colors you have chosen work together? Is the
composition appealing? (A starting-out tip: A strong
centered composition on a square card usually works.)

Remember to ask yourself: what is the purpose
of the project (context), what shape and arrangement
of components (composition) is appropriate, is there
harmonious color, rhythm, and repetition? Take a
moment to step back from your project and determine if the elements are balanced—if the overall feeling is balanced. Or, if not, is there one particular element that is disturbing the balance? Try rotating the
pages and look at them from every angle.

The elements to consider are focal point, contrast, shape, balance. Think about things in a new context: a large object weighs more than a small one. Have you ever thought that color had weight? It does: a bright
color weighs more than a subdued one, an image with a pattern or texture weighs more than one without.

We talk alot about balance in a layout. There are two kinds of balance to consider in your layouts:
symmetrical and asymmetrical. Symmetrical balance is stable and structured. It is classic; a quality you
will find in most formal wedding invitations, for example. And even though it is rooted in fixed princi-
ples, it can be modified slightly. Although a symmetrical design is often the same on each side of a cen-

▲ *A sleek 1930's design presented in a sleek 1930's mauve and
purple palette is powerful with its asymmetrical, off-center layout. The black line etching is the focus. Card by Hero Arts.*

ter line, symmetrical balance can be achieved with elements that are not exactly the same on either side of center, as long as they occupy the same visual space on your layout.

Asymmetrical balance brings contrast, excitement, motion, and informality to a layout. Asymmetrical design demands a bit more planning than a straightforward symmetrical layout, with very engaging results. You can create asymmetrical balance by arranging elements of different sizes, in different quantities, and in different positions. You might place one flower on the right side of the page, and three smaller flowers on the left, or one solid flower on the right and three outline flowers on the left. The visual elements of different sizes and color can balance each other. Shifting the focal point and embellishments off center is another way to create asymmetrical balance. Each element in a layout has weight, size, and color. To achieve asymmetrical balance, determine how much or how little of each element will balance other elements on the layout. For example, a small dark element will balance a much larger lighter element. Rubber stamps are either solid images or outline shapes.

No one notices when a layout is balanced, but when it is not, nothing else will make the page work.

◀ *Three stamped pots of flowers by Nathalie Métivier offer a beautifully orchestrated color palette. The images arranged across the card are enhanced with colored pencil and layered on coordinating papers. The texture added by the maruyama paper and the torn and colored paper beneath adds further dimension. The design is beautifully rendered and completed with embellishments of color, textured-and-torn paper.*

▲ This appealing scrapbook page by Adrienne Kennedy looks like a well-wrapped package from a far-off place. Everything is filled with motion: the dog hanging out the car window, the text panels lifting off the page, the twine wrapping the page, the tree brad. The asymmetric page is balanced. The large light-colored text panel at the bottom balances and supports the large photograph at the top.

COLOR

Color is magic. It can make a layout dance, skip, soothe, or charm. And it's the easiest way to express your personal style, communicate the mood and emotion of the artwork, and establish a relationship between elements on a page or card. Experiment and play with color; it is fun and a quick way to boost your confidence and enthusiasm. The inks, markers, stamp pads, and colored pencils available today give you a tremendous world of color possibilities. Choosing harmonious colors is the challenge.

A color wheel helps you meet that challenge with ease. Using a color wheel helps to take the guesswork out of selecting and combining colors. The sequence of colors on a color wheel is based on the order in which color appears in the spectrum of light, from the shortest wavelength to the longest. It is intriguing to work with shades (color plus black) and tints (color plus white) of one color, with complementary colors (directly opposite colors on the color wheel), and with analogous colors (pairs of colors that are adjacent on the color wheel).

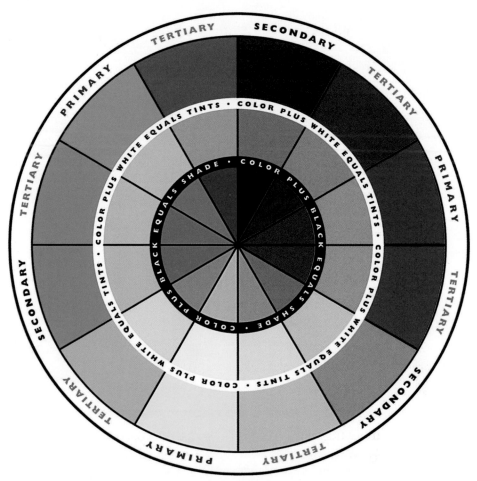

*A monochromatic color scheme uses one color in different values.
Card by Hero Arts.*

▶ *A warm colorful palette, a bouquet of stamped flowers embellished with five red eyelet hearts and a jaunty ribbon add up to a cheery "thank you" note.*

The three primary colors—red, yellow, and blue— are the colors from which all other colors are made. The three secondary colors, made from mixing the primary colors, are orange (made from red and yellow), green (made from blue and yellow), and purple (made from blue and red). The six tertiary (or intermediate) colors are made from mixing one primary color with one secondary color. They are red-orange, yellow-green, blue-violet, red-violet, yellow-orange, and blue-green. Some color schemes look natural together. They are harmonious. These acknowledged color schemes work together: complementary colors (colors opposite each other on the color wheel),triads (three colors spaced equally apart on the color wheel), and split complementary (a color and the two colors next to its complement on the color wheel. Analogous colors (colors next to each other on the color wheel) blend well together.

Think of the colors you are using in this proportion: a gallon for your main color, a quart for your supporting color(s), and an ounce for accents.

PAPER

Paper is glorious, irresistible, tactile. The texture, weight, and color of paper stimulate our senses. It is as important an element to rubber stampers as images and color. Put a sheet of paper in front of paper crafters and, guaranteed, they will pick up the paper, run their fingers across it, hold it up the light to check the surface, comment on the texture or "tooth" and weight. Paper is that irresistible.

Try samples of papers before buying large quantities. See what you like and what you will have use for. There are so many possible combinations of papers. Find the ones that you like, and work with them.

Papers accept ink in their own way. Cardstock will probably be the center of your paper collection. It is available in lots of colors and patterns, sizes, and surfaces. Easy to use, uncoated cardstock works with all inks. Text papers, lighter than cardstock, come in a variety of stationery-appropriate weights.

Text papers are also great for layering, and for making envelopes. Brown kraft paper, and plain bond papers are excellent surfaces for stamping. Look at the stunning wrapping paper created with brown kraft paper we have included in the last chapter.

One of our favorites papers, though, is vellum, available in plain white, or in colors and patterns.

Learn a few basics about design and color, and inks and paper, and then let yourself go and have fun. Crafting is an antidote to the rush and pressure of our lives. If you can't or don't enjoy it, it is only one more task.

◄ *Stacey Turechek's cool violet and green palette with a centered design is framed horizontally by a dark ribbon above and a torn channel of paper below revealing smaller versions of the featured flowers peeking through. The outline stamps are left open, clean, and uncluttered.*

▲ A charming white cardstock card by Stacey Turechek, cut into the shape of toddler rompers, is layered with printed yellow vellum. The blouse neckline and romper legs are edged with decorative fabric trim. Flower eyelets, echoing the stamped flower border on the blouse sleeves, hold the straps in place. The design is whimsical and clean, the palette sunny and childlike, the embellishments effective.

▲ Adrienne Kennedy's muted olive and sage green holiday card with gold overtones is a classic statement of balance and proportion. The harmonious —though unexpected— palette; the formal, just-above-center placement of the main elements; the tasteful layered decorative paper, and the restrained embellishments create a holiday tone poem.

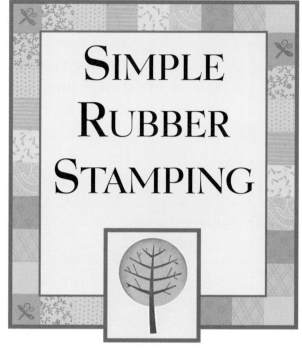

SIMPLE RUBBER STAMPING

Rubber stamping is easy. But the effects are elegant, whimsical, artistic, playful, and even magical. The techniques in this chapter are not difficult to master; some are very simple, others might seem complicated, but usually only because of the addition of an extra element—a ribbon, stitching, folding. Small finishing touches, or embellishments, like these, add striking texture and detail, transforming simple stamped images to elegant finished projects. You are limited only by your imagination. And there is no reason to have a limited imagination!

One thing we would like you to focus on before starting stamping is the ink you will use. There are many varieties of ink pads now available. Knowing what each is suited for will help you get the most out of it and prevent any mishaps with ink that dried too quickly or not at all! Dye ink is transparent, dries quickly on paper surfaces, and is good on glossy, as well as matte coated or uncoated cardstock. Pigment ink is opaque, is slow to dry, but leave crisp, clear color. You would use pigment ink to emboss an image. Chalk ink pads are a hybrid between dye and pigment inks: they are quick drying and can be used on glossy paper (like dye ink is), and the soft chalk finish is opaque (like pigment ink is). Opalite inks produce a shimmering pearl-like finish. And finally, solvent-based inks are used for nonporous surfaces like glass or plastic.

Simple Stamping

Although rubber stamping is simple, that doesn't mean it has to look dull or uninteresting. Start with colored paper and choose a coordinating ink for the stamped image. On this page we have lovely soft palettes of white or ivory with blue and green for cardstock, mats, and ink. The two "Thank you" cards are clean and straightforward. The result is simple, quiet, and elegant.

◀ *Creating the project:*

DRAGONFLY by Cindi Nelson.

1. Stamp the dragonfly with moss green ink on ivory cardstock.

2. Stamp the message —"thank you"— centered just below the dragonfly with the same moss green ink

3. Trim the rectangle and mount it on a moss green mat, and then onto a light blue card.

4. Attach some green and clear micro beads on the dragonfly body to to create dimension.

◀ *Creating the project:*

A SIMPLE THANK YOU by Cindi Nelson.

1. Stamp the striped background design in blue ink on white cardstock.

2. When the ink is dry, stamp the flowers over the background, and draw the green stems.

3. When this layer is dry, stamp the banner in the same blue ink.

4. Center the stamped image on a blue mat, leaving about $1/8$ inch all around the white stamped cardstock. Add two blue mini brads.

5. Mount the matted design on a moss green card.

TIP

It's best to ink a stamp by holding it in one hand with the image up and applying the color (whether ink pad, dauber, or marker) to the raised portions of the image. Keep a light touch to avoid stray ink.

▶ **LADYBUG** by Dave Brethauer. A dainty ladybug glistens with dew as she steps across an isolated feather-like leaf. The dew is created by clear lacquer painted over the stamped and colored shape. Green and red mats hold the ladybug in place on a background of scattered stamped leaves. She is centered on her own panel and on the colorful mats, which are placed off-center, creating a fluid feeling of motion.

▶ **BUTTERFLY BLOCKS** by Lara Zazzi. A luscious raspberry simple floral background pattern is over-stamped with a butterfly and the word "love" in a soft brown ink. The butterfly, poised to take flight, reaches off the top edge of the stamped background block, while the "l" of the word "love" reaches off the card at the opposite corner, creating an immediate pull of energy.

FRAME IT

Mats add visual interest to a card or project. With well-chosen colors, mats frame the image, focusing your attention on the featured element while providing a strong support. These cards are simple, each using a strong mat to provide balance.

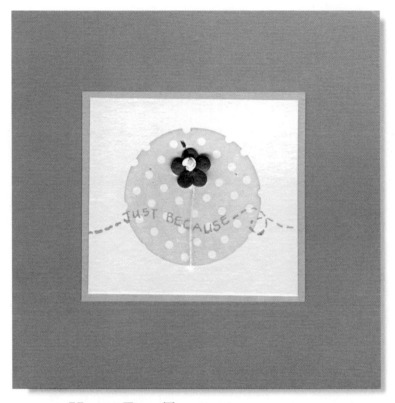

◄ **JUST BECAUSE** by Cindi Nelson. You can create good balance with color. We've used two inks here; one soft blue and one soft green. And we've used two stamps: the circle is stamped in blue, and the message —JUST BECAUSE—is stamped in green. And, finally, we've used two papers plus the basic white cardstock. The little flower embellishment adds a delightful touch. The effect is clean and well balanced.

► **HEART-FELT THANKS** by Katrina Cunningham. A symphony of greens—light, medium, and dark—provide the platform for a rhythmic row of hearts, a red one surrounded by four bright pink ones. The simple black stamped "thank you" placed at the bottom of the page completes the picture.

► **A BOUQUET OF HEARTS** by Kim Smith. The flower heart bouquet is stamped over a soft, monochromatic background. The meandering message lends an informal note. The pink ribbon wrapped around the stems adds dimension and a charming touch.

◄ **CLEAR VASES** by Dave Breathauer. The vases and flowers were inked with waterproof ink. The flowers, stems, and single leaf were colored with watercolor after the stamped image dried. The fluttering butterfly, a separate image, is stamped, colored, cut out, and mounted on the card with foam mounting tape to add dimension.

Solid stamps need no additional coloring to create a dramatic effect, while outline stamps can be filled in with colored pencil, chalk, or watercolor.

sunny days

An image can be stamped in color, or color can be added after stamping the image. We love good colored pencils, a worthwhile investment. The choice of colors for mats here is just as light and cheerful as the images themselves. Our spirits are instantly lifted whenever we look at these two cards.

◀ **SUNNY DAYS** by Katrina Cunningham. These little sandals were stamped with summertime colors, guaranteed to evoke memories of refreshing sherbets. They make you wish you had a pair in every color! The card, image, and mat colors are as relaxed and sunny as the best of summer days. We took special care aligning the three pair of sandals. We stamped a pastel background circle first, and then stamped the sandals on top of the circles. It might help to mark a guide on the cardstock to help you align the images. It is easiest to align the row by stamping the middle image first. It is always wise to stamp on some scrap paper when planning the card.

◀ **BIRTHDAY TIME** by Dave Brethauer. This mat complements the sunny tones of the stamped images. Experiment and find the palette you like.

▼ **COLORFUL CHICKS** by Dave Brethauer. Fun and irresistible, these little chicks with their balloons bring a smile to our faces every time we see them! They are stamped with black ink on white card stock, and then brightened with colored pencils. Using colored pencils on the cardstock allows for the subtle shading of the chicks, hat, and balloons.

TIP

Sometimes mats with large borders are great, but remember that there are times, many times, when a narrow border/mat is just perfect. Look at the size of these mats!

▲ **BOWL OF FLOWERS** by Dave Brethauer. There are so many ways to add color to your cards and pages. Colored pencil is one we reach for often. A simple, single image stamped in black ink on white cardstock turns into something beguiling when you add a melange of bright, cheerful colors with colored pencils. The soft shaded tone in the robin's-egg-blue bowl was created with colored pencils.

▲ **ENTWINED HEARTS.** Another intriguing color application is pearlescent watercolor applied with a brush—here in two colors: pink and purple. No mat this time, but a window is cut into the shimmery top cardstock for us to look through to the charming arrangement. A silver glitter pen highlights the flower centers.

▲ **A TRIO OF FLOWERS.** These velvety-soft simple stamped flowers are also colored with pencils, using a quiet palette. The gray shadow on the vase is created with light watercolor. The added texture of the purple and ivory ribbon decorated with a small pewter buckle adds visual interest. Every one of the colors is included in the multi-layered mats.

▲ **HAPPY VALENTINE'S DAY** by Kim Smith. Two stamps, two colors; one image inside the other creates a magical feeling. Stamp the violet floral heart first, and then the deckled edge in brown around the heart. The brown ink is repeated in the brown mat and type, and the violet ink is echoed in the lovely soft ribbon bow tied at the center of the heart. The not-necessarily-traditional palette is pleasing.

EASY FRAMES

There are any number of ways to frame a stamped image. How about stamping on a metal-rimmed or fluted tag, a decorative device on its own, to create an instant framed image? And then, of course, you might try layering a stamped tag on a mat. Experiment!

◄ **THINKING OF YOU** by Kim Smith. The tag with a single flower image is stamped in one color and attached to the card with glue. A jaunty two-sided ribbon (violet on one side, and green on the other) ties it all together.

◄ **PINK BUTTERFLY.** The pink butterfly is stamped on white cardstock. Punch the cardstock with a deckle-edge square and mount it on a slightly larger square of coordinating paper before placing it on the green leafy card. The row of bright pink sequins defines the upper and lower areas of the card.

► **SPRING.** This spring chick looks ready for anything—perhaps an Easter parade! Stamped on the tag in black and then colored using a marker, the "diamond" pin dresses her up beautifully. The tag is tied to a mat and then layered onto the cardstock. The ends of the ribbon are tucked behind the tag and through the eyelets. Six small rectangles are punched from various colored papers, all coordinated with the striped paper serving as the large mat, and mounted onto a white mat. A letter—to spell SPRING—is centered in each rectangle.

birthday wishes

HAPPY BIRTHDAY

▲▲**BIRTHDAY WISHES** by Lara Zazzi. One simple image stamped on a metal-rimmed tag decorates the card. The smaller tag is mounted on a patterned mat, the larger one stands alone. Each is tied to its card with a jaunty decorative-edged ribbon. Either way, the tag is an effective frame presenting the featured image with style. The color choices are appealing; cool tones (blues) for one, and warm tones (yellows) for the other.

FRAMING VARIETY

Each of these cards has an interesting frame. In one we look through a window in the top layer to see the stamped image. In another, a frame is created with a ric-rac-bordered mat, and in a third, the bottom half of the front of the card is removed and the scalloped edge frames the stamped image. All frames, but a substantially different look for each of them.

◄ **DOUBLE WINDOW** by Kim Smith. We used double-faced paper (light on one side, dark on the other) for this wonderful simple stamped card. The stamping is easy, but the card itself is a little tricky in the folding.

Creating the project:

1. Stamp the flower in a soft brown ink once on the light side of the paper. Trim a square and set aside.

2. Stamp a column of flowers the height of the card in brown ink. Trim the paper to about 1 ½ inches wide with the stamped column on the paper's right edge. Fold in half horizontally.

3. To create the card, measure a piece of the two-sided paper three times the width of the card. Fold the card in thirds horizontally, so that the front of the card is double thickness, and there is a fold on each side of the front. (See the template on page 130.) You will then have a dark side facing up; beneath the dark side there will be a light side facing up. Punch a small square window in the second layer of the card. Trace the punched square through the window onto the back of page 1. Punch a slightly larger square in the front page, from the back, centering the traced square image. You now have a window with a light color border around it.

4. Center the single square with the stamped flower you created in step 1 in the middle of the window, and glue it down.

5. Glue the column of stamped flowers down the left edge of the card front, with the blank half of the strip to the back.

6. Stamp the message along the bottom of the card front.

▲ **HANG UP** by Kim Smith. The little dress and hangar are stamped and enhanced with colored pencil and then mounted on a dark brown ribbed paper square. The delicate pink ric-rac border supporting the brown textured mat is a delightful touch. It echoes the pink edge of the dress, and seemingly lifts the mat right off the card. The composition is simple, centered, and straightforward. How about the color? What color cardstock would you have used?

▲ **SPRING TREE** by Dave Brethauer. First we stamped the green circle, and then the bare tree on top of it. We added the mini red lights for a festive touch. The scalloped edge of the cut front window acts like a stage curtain and presents the featured image. The materials are simple, the stamping is simple, but the imaginativeness here is far from simple. Remember to take the time to quietly look at your materials and see them in a new way.

BACKGROUNDS SAY IT

Bright colored mats supporting bright colored stamped images create a celebratory feeling, especially when added decorative elements repeat the colors. But it is the background color that sets the stage, whether it be the red and white of Christmas holiday, or the brilliant orange of a crisp autumn day.

◄ **HAPPY HOLIDAYS** by Hero Arts. This fun-loving holiday card is finished with colored pencil and a bright red crayon outlining the window. The colorful row of mini buttons underlines the window much like footlights on a stage.

▼ **MERRY AND BRIGHT.** Bright, crisp cardstock in Christmas colors create a joyful feeling. The three Christmas lights are stamped on white cardstock, colored with markers, finished with a clear gloss coating, and hung on a silver thread "wire." The silver-star ornaments attached to the printed red ribbon add a festive note. The ingenious mat on the card far left is made by folding a loop of ribbon and placing it between the bottom mat and the red card. It echoes the shape of the Christmas tree.

► **AUTUMN.** This scrapbooking page, with a background prepared by Jan Williams, shouts autumn, Halloween, and the joy of childhood. Color has done its job here. Who is to say: are the colors of the page drawn from the colors in the photograph or was the photograph chosen to complementthe autumnal page theme?

Save your scraps and leftover Christmas package ribbons for future card projects.

AUTUMN

just ducky!

▲ **JUST DUCKY.** A Muse Art Stamps. This bright little ducky is happy as a lark strolling under his umbrella. The stamping is simple, although four stamps were used to create the scene. The narrow mat echoes the color of the umbrella. And that rain is downright cheerful! The off-center placement is perfect.

▲ **EASTER EGG** by Kim Smith. A simple stamped egg is studded with micro pearls and wrapped with a mini ribbon. Further texture is added with the floral pattern on the egg. We cut slits in either side of the egg to insert the ribbon between the white cardstock and the blue-green mat. The matted stamped image is layered onto a muted checkerboard card.

◄ **THANKS A BUNCH.** An unusual shape to the central panel creates interest. The bunch of glitzy flowers and leaves are colored with glitter pens. The message is stamped in black and the stitching lines are drawn in black. The orange and pink layers are tied together with a brown and white polka-dot ribbon.

▶ **THE WORDS HAVE IT** by Adrienne Kennedy. A quiet palette—soft blue and white—is highlighted with black type. Busy paper patterns, but a simple palette contribute to a peaceful effect. The three tags are lifted off the card with mounting tape and highlighted with soft decorative ribbon bows.

▼ **TRIP TO THE ZOO.** A simple tri-fold picture frame is personalized to refresh memories of a favorite trip to the zoo. The frame is first painted and then stamped with leaves in a few autumnal shades. The word "safari" is stamped in a complementary color down the left-hand side. The little giraffe charm and bright tassels add dimension and spots of color.

greetings

◄ **THREE POTS OF FLOWERS** by Kim Smith. This simple card is stamped, colored with color pencil, trimmed, and layered.

Creating the Project:

1. Stamp the image in black. Apply color with color pencil.

2. Trim the edges and apply color to the edge with a gold glitter pen.

3. Mount the stamped layer to blue cardstock. Insert brads through the four corners of the stamped image and the blue mat.

4. Attach the two layers to the striped background and then to the green card.

5. Stamp the greeting below the striped mat.

GARDEN PARTY

One charming stamp is used for four related projects by Kim Smith. You can coordinate a variety of projects with a single stamp, a similar palette, and a little imagination. The place card has a tumbling tower of block stamps cleverly reaching above the fold line. The three tags are cut out and tied individually in a column on the gift bag

Creating the Project:

▶ **INVITATION**

1. Print the invitation from your computer on ivory cardstock, using computer fonts, leaving room at the top of the card for the stamped images.

2. Stamp the three small images (one stamp)in black ink, and add color with colored pencil.

3. Mount the invitation on two layers of cardstock of pleasing colors.

Although the three shaped-tag topiaries are actually one stamp, it is used that way only once for this project. The rest of the time, the topiaries are cut apart and each is used separately.

Creating the Project:

▼ PLACE CARDS

1. To create the place card, ink and stamp one of the images at a jaunty tilt partially above the fold line at the left center of the card. Put a mask over it and stamp the second image just below it. Color the stamped images with the same colored pencils you used on the invitation.

2. Mount a piece of ivory cardstock on a slightly larger sized piece of green cardstock. Cut the right side of the two stamped images from $1/8$ inch below the fold line to about $1/8$ inch above the bottom of the place card. Insert the layered smaller card behind the stamped images, and glue to the place card.

3. Cut around the portion of the stamped image that is above the fold line to let it stand silhouetted above the card when the card is placed on the table.

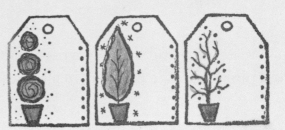

Please Join Us For A
Garden Party

Sat. April 28th

1:00pm

251 Main Street
Fairfield

RSVP by April 20th

555-3344

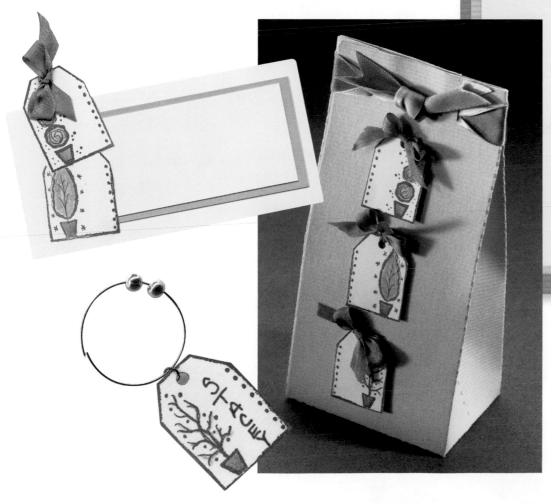

ONE STAMP, THREE PROJECTS

※

Create a colorful summer garden with one stamp and two ink colors. The repetition of this luscious pink daisy is irresistible. In all cases, we have added green accents and more pink decoration.

Creating the project:

GIFT WRAPPED PACKAGE by Kim Smith.

1. Cut a piece of plain white paper large enough to wrap the package tightly.

2. Ink the large daisy stamp with two colors of ink—one color for the petals, and one for the center.

3. Randomly stamp the surface of the paper with the daisy, re-inking as necessary. Vary the direction of the image to have some motion to the surface. Stamp and silhouette three extra flowers for decoration. Wrap the gift.

4. Tie a complementary color ribbon around the package and secure with tape. Layer the three silhouetted

flowers in a pleasing pattern as a package topper over the taped ribbon.

5. Fold summer green ribbon into leaves as shown and insert under the silhouetted package topper.

Creating the Project:

▶ **GIFT CARD** by Kim Smith.

1. To create the gift card, stamp the flower on white cardstock.

2. Stamp the message across the bottom portion of the petals in brown ink.

3. Wrap a deep rose ribbon around a green mat slightly larger than the cardstock. Mount the stamped cardstock onto the green mat, and layer on two more mats .

Creating the Project:

▶ **SCRAPBOOK PAGE**

1. To create the 8 x 8-inch scrapbook page, mat your photograph on two layers of complementary-colored green mats. Add soft green ribbon photo corners to two diagonal corners and a silhouetted pink daisy to the top right corner.

2. Attach the mounted photo to a shell pink page.

3. Punch four each medium green and light green deckle-edge squares. Mount the smaller squares on top of the larger ones. Stamp the word "love", one letter per square, in pink. Tuck another stamped pink daisy under the left corner of the matted photograph.

DAD'S DAY

✹

Cards for Dad for Father's Day and Valentine's Day. Brown reigns supreme on these more masculine cards.

◀ **A VALENTINE FOR DAD** by Adrienne Kennedy. The palest pink, really a beige-pink is stamped with black letters and mounted on black mats. The textured heart is stamped in black, centered in a square frame. A black ribbon ties it all together. Three basic layers, plus the foam mounted LOVE down the left side, completes the card.

◀ **A BOX FOR DAD** by Kelly Carolla. A simple box is covered in beige paper stamped in coordinating colors and enhanced with colored pencil. A few colorful butterflies fly across the field. Sponged textured paper lines the recessed panel on the top of the box. A small stamped square provides the mat for a dried flower.

▶ **DAD'S SHOE CARD** by Adrienne Kennedy. Complete with leather tie, the shoe shape is stamped with all sorts of shoe messages ("If the shoe fits," "Kick up your heels." "Wears like an old shoe."). The image is mounted on brown striped paper, brown patterned paper, and then on brown cardboard stamped with the message.

◀ **DAD'S BIRTHDAY CARD** by Adrienne Kennedy. A distressing stamp is the base, combined with a letter stamp. The squares are trimmed and mounted on medium brown squares, and then mounted on a distressed card layered with medium brown paper and paper printed with an old map. The alphabet squares march diagonally down the card.

TIP

To create a distressed look, tap and feather the edges of the cardstock with an inkpad.

FRAMED AND LAYERED

❋

Create marvelous frames and a center image from one marvelous stamp. This project was created by Nathalie Métivier from Magenta Rubber Stamps.

1. Stamp the large image twice. Cut only the center flower of one image. Set aside. Cut the second image around the outside edge.

2. Center a 2-inch square of cardboard on the large trimmed image and cut around it, using the cardboard as a template, to remove a square piece. You now have a frame shape and a square shape. Color the edges of the 2-inch square cardboard and mount the stamped square on it. Mount the frame on dark green cardstock, and then on ivory cardstock mats. Attach the small square on the mounted frame.

3. Attach the previously cut flower (see Step 1) on the flower in the center of the 2-inch square with mounting tape.

4. Stamp the edges of a dark green card with a lighter green ink, using the smaller vine stamp. Mount the layered frame onto the card. Decorate the green panel behind the diamond-shaped center with Magenta Peel-Off's. Add dimension to the center flower by pushing into the center of it with eraser end of a new pencil and pulling the leaves up around it.

◄ ▼ **PINK FRAME-IN-A-FRAME CARD AND ENVELOPE.** by Nathalie Métivier. The large card is made with one large stamp. The image is stamped twice, cut into frames, and reassembled. An old-fashioned, nostalgic look that will please your romantic friends. The envelope flap has a clever twist. The central flower hides another flower underneath it which slips into a slit cut into the envelope to hold the envelope closed.

1. Stamp the large image on two complementary colored printed papers—light pink and deeper rose.

2. With a mat knife and straight-edge ruler, cut out the center panel and each frame from both stamped papers.

3. Mount the frames and panels, alternating colors. Silhouette the central flower image and leaves from the light pink stamped paper and attach to the center of the card.

4. To create the envelope, stamp the panel stamp twice in dark rose ink on patterned paper. (See the envelope template on page 128.) Cut the center flower only from one and set aside. Cut out the second stamped image. Cut a slit in the envelope so you can tuck the trimmed flower at the center of the panel into it to close the envelope. Glue the upper half of the single flower on top of the one on the panel. Leave the bottom half of the top flower loose so it will cover the flower underneath it when that one is tucked into the slit. Decorate the panel with Peel-Offs silver decorative accents.

TIP

Peel-Off's can be used as positive or negative shapes. To take a positive shape, just lift it. If necessary, use the pointed tip of a craft knife. To gather the negative pieces, it is best to use adhesive tape. Press hard to make all the pieces you need adhere to the tape. Peel-Off's are easily repositionable on cardstock. You can move them around to find the right composition.

EMBOSSING

You can create an elegant, raised image on a card by heat embossing or dry embossing. When you emboss with heat, firs t stamp the image and then sprinkle embossing powder on it. After heating, the image becomes raised and shiny, a sophisticated, professional-looking result.

Pigment inks are best to use for embossing because they are slow-drying. Embossing ink, clear and tinted, is available in pads or dauber-topped bottles. Embossing pens are available in many colors, with fine, calligraphic, and brush tips.

Many types of embossing powders are available, and each produces a different effect. Clear embossing powder enhances the color of the ink, while raising it and adding shine. Metallic and colored embossing powders will cover the ink, changing the color. Tinsel powders add sparkle. New embossng powders are introduced regularly.

To properly melt the embossing powder you need a heat source of at least 300 degrees Fahrenheit. A heat gun is the easiest and most effecive tool, but you could use a toaster, an iron set on "cotton," or an oven set at 300 degrees Fahrenheit. A hair dryer will not get hot enough to use for embossing.

Dry embossing is a simple process of tracing an image with a template under the cardstock or paper. The pressure of your touch pushes the shape into the paper . The template can be made of brass or plastic. If the cardstock is face down, the image will be raised from the surface; if you place the cardstock face up, the finished image will be depressed into the paper. Either way, you have added elegant texture.

JUST BECAUSE

EMBOSSING

Embossing, dry or wet, produces a stunning dimensional touch. Dry embossing produces a raised image with or without color. Place a template face up on a lightbox or other light source (a bright window would work) with the paper on the template. Using a ball burnisher or embossing tool, gently push the paper or cardstock into the recessed template image. Keep the embossing tool against the image outline as you trace the shape.

◄ **DRAGONFLIES IN FLIGHT** by Kim Smith. These three handsome dragonflies in flight were dry-embossed using a simple PVC template, producing a subtle, elegant effect. The dragonflies were embossed on the green cardstock in alternating directions, one above the other, and then trimmed to the appropriate size and mounted on a slightly larger mat of white cardstock, and layered onto the blue card. The message "Just because" is stamped down the right side of the card.

▼ **BUTTERFLY** by Kim Smith. The sparkling look of this butterfly is not difficult to achieve. Again, we used a simple PVC template shape. If you wax the back side of the paper, the embossing tool will slide freely over the paper and produce a smooth line.

Creating the project:

1. Dry emboss the butterfly on soft violet cardstock.
2. Gently remove the color from the raised image with fine sandpaper. You now have a white raised line on the violet cardstock.
3. Highlight the inner edge of the butterfly shape, and add the tips of the antennae with a glitter pen.
4. Trim the embossed violet cardstock into a tag shape and punch a hole at the top.
5. Stamp the grass along the bottom of a green card.
6. Attach the tag off-center with a green check ribbon, just above the stamped grass. Add the message.

THINKING OF YOU

TIP

Before heating, dust off any particles of emboss-ing powder that have migrated and stuck to unwanted areas on your card or project.

▶ **EMBOSSED SWAN** by Marie-France Perron. The outline of this fabulous swan is embossed with ink and then bedecked with feathers. The soft, natural palette allows the bird to dominate centerstage. The body of the swan is colored with an easy watercolor technique.

Creating the Project:

1. Stamp the swan on white cardstock using a midnight blue inkpad.

2. Apply clear embossing powder to the wet ink. Shake off the excess powder before heating with a heat gun to "puff" the image.

3. Scribble some colors with water-based markers on a nonporous surface. Then take a small brush and a little water to grab the color and paint the body of the swan.

4. Tear the bottom edge of the white cardstock and color the edge with coordinated color ink.

5. Tear and enhance the bottom edge of a larger rectangular piece of blue-green cardstock. Fold the top down about ⅝ inch. Insert the white card under the flap and pierce a hole about ¼ inch in from each side. Thread a mint green ribbon through the holes and tie in front.

6. Stamp aqua paper with a script text stamp in blue ink.

7. Layer the papers and attach them to a green card.

8. Add the swan's blue feathers.

Using the embossing to resist ink is an interesting technique, producing elegant results. The embossed areas of the paper will not accept paint or ink, so you can paint over the whole surface after embossing the selected spots and then wipe the surface to remove the color from the embossed images. Clear embossing ink preserves the color of your paper.

▼ **EMBOSSED MOSAIC** by Kim Smith The four small embossed squares fit together like a graceful mosaic.

1. Ink the two flower stamps (one solid, and one open) with clear embossing ink. Stamp the two flower images.

2. Cover the stamped image with clear embossing powder. Tap off the excess powder and heat with a heat gun to melt the embossing powder.

3. Cover the entire card surface with rose colored ink, right over the clear embossed images.

4. Remove the ink from the embossed areas by wiping gently with a dry, soft cloth or tissue. Punch two squares from each stamped image. Mount on a black mat, and layer onto a white mat and maroon card.

1.

2.

3.

4.

▶ **SUNSET** by Kim Smith. We used watercolor on this elegant card to encourage a natural-looking streaked sunset sky. Stamp the flower eight times with clear embossing ink in an interesting arrangement of varying heights across white cardstock. Emboss with clear embossing powder. Paint the sunset sky over the surface with watercolors. Wipe with a soft, dry cloth or tissue to reveal the white flowers against the sky.

TIP

Remember to collect and save the excess embossing powder for future projects. Just sprinkle the powder on the stamped image and then tilt the card and gently tap the excess powder into an envelope or jar for safe-keeping.

▲ **GOLD EMBOSSED HEART.** The four heart stamps used in this project were designed to be used with a heart punch. That's irresistible! And the small box package is irresistible. The four hearts are stamped on light pink paper with clear embossing ink and embossed with gold embossing powder. They are then punched out with the coordinating heart punch. The box is tied with a soft pink organza ribbon with a loose bow on the top, and one heart is positioned on each side of a small gift box. Makes one wonder what is inside!

◀ **4 LEAVES, 1 STAMP**
by Kim Smith. All four of
these intriguing gold
embossed outline leaf
images are on one stamp.
The image is stamped in
clear embossing ink on
flecked green paper.
Sprinkle with gold
embossing powder;
shake off the excess
powder and heat with a
heat gun to raise the surface. The embossed
image is trimmed and
layered onto succes-
sively larger mats of co-
ordinated colors.
Notice the ribbon
slipped between two
layers of the mats,
adding an interesting note.

HAPPY BIRTHDAY

◀ **GOLDEN SEASHELLS.** The four seashells
are stamped with clear embossing ink and heat
embossed in gold. A charming extra touch
with this project is the flip-flop sandals that are
stamped (the stamp is a pair of sandals), colored, and cut apart and arranged artistically on
the top layer of this card. We added a punched
flower and special jewel to decorate the sandals. The palette is consistent: the decorative
ric-rac echoes the sand color of the flip flops,
the bottom background paper, and the gold
seashells. The stamped greeting echoes the
dark ric-rac.

▶ **MADE WITH LOVE** by Nathalie Métivier. This whole image—two upright blocks and one horizontal block—is one stamp that is stamped on ivory cardstock in a red ink, and then embossed with tinsel embossing powder.

Creating the Project:

1. Stamp the image on ivory cardstock using a deep red ink.
2. Color the stamped image with colored pencil.
3. When the ink is really dry, redraw the frames and some hearts with a small brush and clear embossing ink and emboss with tinsel embossing powder.
4. Trim the stamped image with decorative-edged scissors.
5. Mount on a vellum rectangle.
6. Stamp a soft pink cardstock with a dictionary definition (love is the definition) stamp in a deep rose. Tear and lightly color the edges of the paper.
7. Layer the vellum onto the stamped pink mat, using foam mounts to lift it off the paper.
8. Add a Peel Off's gold frame around the vellum mat. Layer onto two more successively-larger mats, one enhanced with metallic dots around the rim, the final one with a deckled edge .

TIP

To create soft edge effects, or shading, in your stamped projects, try to soften the stamped lines with a colored pencil. You can smudge and gently rub the color to create perfect shadows.

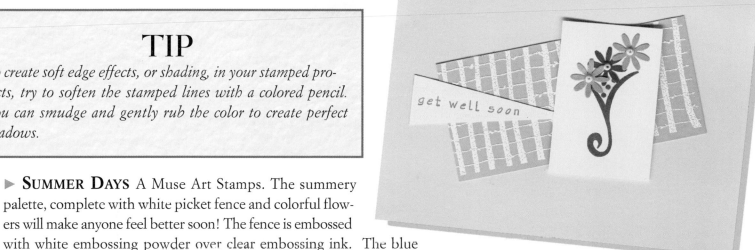

▶ **SUMMER DAYS** A Muse Art Stamps. The summery palette, complete with white picket fence and colorful flowers will make anyone feel better soon! The fence is embossed with white embossing powder over clear embossing ink. The blue type echoes the summer blue sky behind the fence, and the flowers sit jauntily in the summer-grass green vase. The upward angle of the fence adds a lilting "feel good" note.

► **SILVER BELL** by Adrienne Kennedy. The words are in the shape of a bell. You just have to stamp them and then cut the bell shape. The sophisticated palette is all ivory and silver. There are three underlying layers to the card. The bottom layer is stamped randomly with text in silver ink, stamping several times with one inking so that the image has a deliberately uneven and "antiqued" look. The next layer up from the bottom is embossed vellum, followed by embossed matte paper held in place with four silver photo corners. The stamped and silver embossed bell is affixed using foam mounts to lift it off the page.

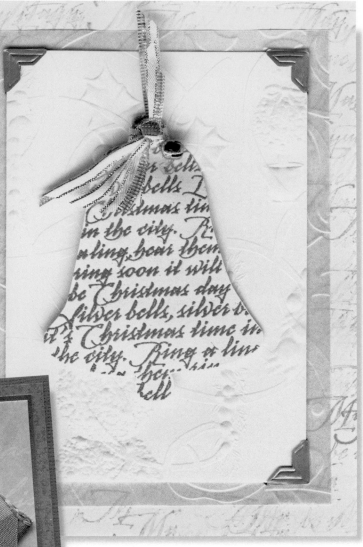

TIP
Try using a deckle ruler to create a wave of layered deckle edges.

◄ **AUTUMN LEAVES.** The colors of an autumn afternoon range from green to copper to violet and brown. The gold embossed leaves (one stamp) are gathered with an elegant coordinated ribbon tied at a corner edge. The underlying deckle-edged papers are elegantly layered.

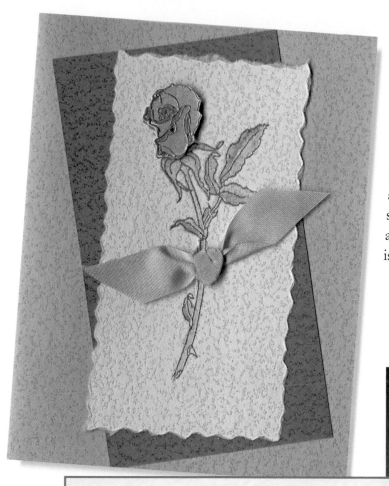

◄ **A Single Rose.** A soft summer-garden feeling is created with a two-toned rose and greenery mounted on soft blue-green mats—cool and delicious. The gold-embossed edges to the flower outline add an elegant touch. The flower was stamped twice and embossed in gold. The color was added with watercolor. Silhouette the petals of one of the flowers and layer on top of the complete image using foam mounting tape. The two mats are tilted to create a feeling of movement in the summer breeze as well as the natural shape of the rose stem. The light and dark mats and the deckled edge add interest and movement. The crystal dew drop on the rose is a finishing touch.

TIP

Use a firm metal brush to lengthen the fibers of the torn edges for a softer, fibrous effect.

▶ **Wedding Gift.** This elegant package is wrapped simply with co-ordinating violet-colored paper and ribbons. The bride-and-groom image is stamped twice: once on the large cardstock tag, and once on the vellum overlay. The stamped image is colored on the cardstock and embossed on the vellum, creating a dreamlike effect. The message is stamped in violet ink on the vellum.

Thinking of you tickles my toes!

HAPPY FATHER'S DAY

hello friend

THANK YOU

PUNCHING, FOLDING & TEARING

Punches are mini-, hand-held paper cutters. And if you learn the secret of paper crafters—that is, to turn the punch upside-down to frame the image you want to punch—you will turn out marvelous, professional-looking punch-art projects. Perfect shape every time, with crisp, clean edges and no cutting around one side to even out the shape! Even the simplest punched shapes have a lot of potential: they can be layered, cut, colored, and combined to create complex designs.

Folded paper is endlessly fascinating. The extra texture and dimension add instant drama to a card or scrapbook page. We have included examples of several different folding techniques from origami to iris folding, tea-bag folding as well as old-fashioned pleating and accordion folding.

A single piece of origami paper can be manipulated into an elegant three-dimensional object with a few basic folds. Iris folding, a fascinating technique with folded papers arranged in a spiral pattern, is so-called because the multi-layered piece resembles the iris of a camera. And don't you remember those pleated skirts? Well, you can pleat paper, too.

We can't seem to do enough to paper. We color, bend, fold, tear, and cut it. Paper collage provides a wonderful opportunity to play with color, shape, and texture by tearing, cutting, and layering altered sheets of paper into something new and exciting. Anything can happen. Enjoy it!

ABOUT PUNCHES

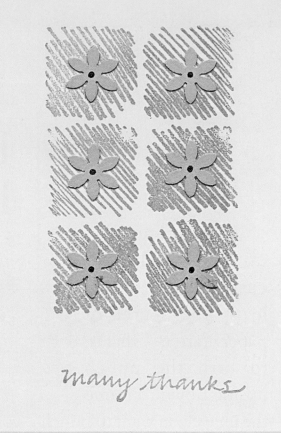

You don't need to own a vast array of punches. One punched shape may be all you need for a special accent on a card, a scrapbook page, or many other paper craft projects. With a punch, you can cut sections of paper in a variety of shapes and patterns. And using just a portion of a punch can produce imaginative results—a delightful floral border for a card or scrapbook page can be created with one small heart punch . Try it. It's fun!

▼ **RHYTHM AND HEART.** You can't go wrong with a simple, straightforward design of pleasing repetitive shapes and harmonious colors. The symmetrical composition of the four small squares (two of light-ribbed pale blue cardstock, and two of coffee colored barely-flecked cardstock) are tied together gracefully with a small heart punched out of shell pink cardstock. The harmonious composition coupled with the harmonious palette conveys a feeling of calm.

▲ **YELLOW DAISIES** by Kim Smith. One simple squiggle stamp, repeated six times in lavender ink, marches down the front of the card two-by-two, creating windowpanes, on top of which are placed six daisies punched out of bright yellow paper. A drop of lavender glitter is applied to the center of each flower with a gel pen, and the greeting is stamped in lavender ink.. The composition is simple and the complementary colors pleasing.

TIP

To keep your punches working smoothly, try punching through wax paper or aluminum foil several times. Or, if your punch is sticky, put it in the freezer for fifteen minutes. The metal will contract slightly, making it easier to punch.

TIP

Keep the parts of the shapes punched out that you are not using immediately. Here we used the negative shape, and saved the positive feet for a future project.

▲ **A Gloved Hand.** A striped background paper dictates the palette used for this card. The card itself is a warm ivory, the large base mat is tan with stripes of yellow, green, blue, and red. The scalloped edges of the blue rectangle draw your eye to the center. The punched gloved hand has been decorated with a "diamond" ring, leather stitching marks, and a wrist decoration made from half of a punched daisy. The tiny button on the wrist reappears in the four corners of the type panel beneath. And the scalloped edges of the panel are echoed in the fluid line of the type.

▶ **Twinkle Toes.** There certainly are lots of new craft materials at hand. Here's an unusual one—a crushed bottle cap. It functions beautifully as a frame for the two baby footprints punched out of sage green cardstock and layered over baby pink cardstock inside the somewhat-smoothed edges of the smashed metal bottle cap. The sage green and pink palette continues with a pink mat sandwiched between two sage green mats, one patterned and one plain. The two-toned pink bow adds a cheerful note. We put a small epoxy circle over the punched shape, like a shadow box.

◄ **PARTY HATS.** The shapes are simple, the design is simple, the colors are simple, and the card is easy to make! You can use the leftover paper after punching the large triangles for the small pieces.

Creating the Project:

1. Punch four triangles as follows: 2 red, 1 blue 1 yellow.
2. Cut one of the red triangles into horizontal stripes and glue them onto the yellow triangle.
3. Punch small circles out of blue, yellow, and white cardstock. and attach them in a random pattern to the red triangle.
4. Punch small stars out of red and yellow cardstock, and attach them to the blue triangle.
5. Attach decorative elements to the top of the triangle: a cotton ball, ribbon, or heart brad.
6. Stamp and emboss the words.

TIP

To get a dimensional look when adding small objects to a larger one, try placing some slightly off the edge of the large object, and trim them flush with the edge. Look at the stars and circles on this project. The triangles have become decorated party hats.

► **UNITED WE STAND** by Kim Smith. The composition and the color of this card elicit a response. The rhythmic composition—three red and white hearts spread across the card, strung together with a dark blue ribbon—is almost formal, as is the palette—red, white, and blue on silver, but the artwork is a bit jaunty and informal, more inviting.

▶ **SLIDING INTO HOME** by Donna Volovski. The punching and the folding on this card are interesting. The featured large punched flower is actually attached to the purple tag inside the folded blue envelope, and slides into a slot cut in the blue envelope.

Creating the project:

1. Fold an envelope using the template on page 129. Cut the slit into the top edge of the fold as shown on the template. Fold on the fold lines, but do not glue the envelope together yet.

2. Punch the large pinwheel flower out of white cardstock and color softly with pink chalk. Set aside.

3. Punch various sun, swirl, and flower shapes from several shades of yellow, pink, and white cardstock.

4. Stamp the greeting on the envelope.

5. Layer the punched shapes in a pleasing display, keeping the large pinwheel flower in reserve.

6. Decorate the flowers with a glitter pen.

7. Cut a large tag out of purple cardstock to fit inside the envelope, and slip it inside the envelope to check the placement of the pinwheel flower.

8. Attach the pinwheel to the tag so that it slips down into the slit in the top edge of the card.

9. Add the sheer white ribbon.

TIP

When punching rings like these, punch the smaller circle first, and set aside. Slip the paper with the missing circle into the larger punch. Before punching, turn the punch upside-down to frame the portion to be cut.

◀ **THREE-RING CIRCUS** by Stacey Turechek. Playing with punches like this was great fun—but a lot of work! We punched a series of "bull's-eye" rings with different-sized circle punches out of brown and turquoise paper and layered the rings onto the white card. Each ring in each circle needed two size punches—for the outer and inner edges. That means six punches for each three-ring circle. The Father's Day message is stamped in brown ink on a punched turquoise blue tag.

▲ **PUNCHED, FOLDED, AND CUT** by Kim Smith. A stamped turquoise-blue background sets the stage for the stamped monogram. The small square is then punched with a scalloped edge. Layer the punched monogram square onto note cards with a piece of decorative ribbon layered between the punched square and the card. The ribbon col- ors mimic the colors in the background and alphabet. The scalloped edge of the folded note card echoes the scalloped edge of the small square. Repetition is a succesful design tool. The matchbook cover repeats the scalloped edge on the lower lip. A delightful little gift when you want to bring "something" to a hostess. Note cards always come in handy.

◄ **A SIMPLE WINDOW.** A monogrammed flower viewed through a plain window is decorated with a jauntily tied green and white stripe ribbon. Just the simple design and palette for a short note to a special friend—perhaps in a child's lunch box, or inviting yourself to Grandmother's for tea? The punched flower is shaded with colored chalk, and the initial is stamped in black in the center of the flower. The bow completes the card. All very simple, and a joy to receive. (Note: The window is punched from the right side of the card .)

► **A NEGATIVE BECOMES A POSITIVE.** There are always two versions of a punched shape—the positive (the actual shape cut out) and the negative (the piece left after the positive shape has been removed). The heart is punched out of the pink cardstock here and layered over a purple mat. The tricky part is aligning the words properly on the pink and purple cardstock.

Creating the Project:
1. Stamp the message on pink cardstock.
2. Punch a heart out of pink cardstock, right through some of the words.
3. Stamp the message again on purple cardstock.
4. Align the words through the punched heart and attach the pink paper to the purple paper by putting adhesive on the back of the pink paper.
5. Trim around the purple paper to create a mat.
6. Layer the purple mat onto the polka dot mat and slip into the punched corners of the yellow card.
7. Finish with small pink brads in the corners of the pink paper.

TIP
Wait to cut the purple paper to exact size until after you have attached the pink paper to it. You have to align the type through the punched heart and it would be more difficult to have the purple paper precut.

A CHILD'S DELIGHT

These five projects will delight young children. The compositions are simple, the colors playful, and the repetitive patterns of the images delightful. Not everything has to be stamped when you are creating your own cards. The only stamping on the trucks and nautical cards is the greeting. The little giraffes, however, are stamped and colored and then punched and layered. The trucks are from the negative shapes, while the anchors and boats are the positive shapes, placed on top of the white mats. Remember to save the negative anchor and boat shapes for another project.

◀ **PUNCHED MITT .** Metallic-rimmed tags have become popular additions to cards and scrapbook pages. They bring focus to the elements and add texture to the page. This project is as easy as it gets! Punch the baseball mitt out of brown paper, and center in a tag. Punch the heart out of red paper and place it in the mitt. Add a red and white checked bow to the tag and layer it on to the card. Stamp the big, bold message, and that's it!

◀ **ANCHORS AWEIGH.** A classic, symmetrical, centered design is straightforward and clean. Punch two anchors and one sailboat out of red cardstock. Mount the three positive images onto white punched, deckle-edged cardstock squares. Layer the white squares onto larger navy blue punched squares, and then onto the red card. Stamp the greeting in navy blue ink .

▼ **A TRIO OF TRUCKS.** Punch the trucks first, and then insert each cardstock into the scalloped square punch turning the punch upside-down to position the truck in center of square. Then punch larger scalloped-edge squares for the contrasting punched scalloped-edged mats. Attach tiny buttons for wheels. Stamp "Happy Birthday" below the squares.

HAPPY BIRTHDAY

Happy Easter!

◀ **EASTER BASKET** by Kim Smith. A basket full of stamped and punched Easter eggs is always delightful. The melange of colors in the natural colored basket feel joyful and celebratory. Stamp brown paper and then punch out the basket shape. Stamp various Eastery-colored designs on white paper and then punch egg shapes. We used a border punch for the grass in the basket. We punched the corners of a soft-blue textured mat with a corner punch. "Happy Easter" is stamped in bright pink. The gingham ribbon adds a finishing touch.

▲ **THREE GIRAFFES** by Kim Smith. Stamp three giraffes on white cardstock, leaving lots of room around each one. Color the giraffes with colored pencil and then punch each one out using a scalloped-edge rectangle punch. Punch dark brown rectangles using a slightly larger scalloped-edge rectangle punch for the three mats. The spotted background paper is stamped using a solid circle and an outline punch.

TIP

Use a stamp positioner to position the borders of the solid circle stamped spots.

▲ **CHARMING AND SIMPLE** by Kim Smith. Stamp the vase of flowers in black. Add color with colored pencil in various shades of pink and green. Punch two sizes of flowers out of light pink cardstock and attach them over the colored bouquet for added dimension. Add shine to the vase with a glaze pen and glitter to the flower centers with a glitter pen. The just-fallen single flower at the base of the vase adds a fresh touch.

▲ **IF THE SHOE FITS.** Punch the shoe in light pink and again in dark pink. Trim the dark pink to create a sole for the shoe. Punch various flower shapes to create the bouquet.

TIP

To give dimension to the flowers, use a stylus to gently push the flower shapes into a soft carving eraser or carving block.

▶ **DESIGNER BAGS.** Punch out two bags, one from striped and one from pink cardstock. Cut the latch and handle from the pink cardstock and layer it over the striped bag. Punch out the tag, use a glitter pen to stitch around the rim. Attach the bag and stamp the sentiment. Punch out various flowers and leaves; shape each one and arrange them on the purse.

▶ **FLOWER TAGS** by Kim Smith. Punch and silhouette three pink and two green flowers. Punch two paper circles to fit inside the tags. Add the punched flowers, layer the papers, attach three flowers, and stamp.

◀ **MAIL DELIVERY OF HEARTS.** Stamp the background with "Words of Love," attach a small envelope and fill it with lots of tiny punched hearts delivered from a bird you have also punched out. The green and white grosgrain ribbon is sandwiched between the mats to give the feeling of a mailbox flag.

TIP
It helps to use a pointed-end tweezer when building and stacking punched shapes.

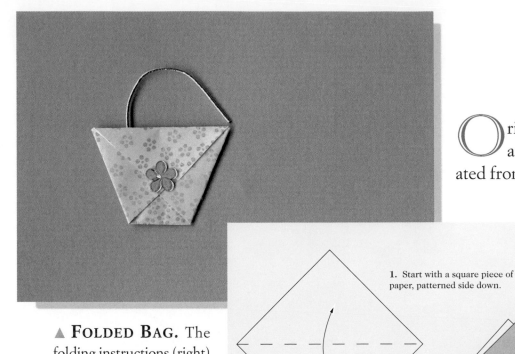

FOLDING

O rigami, the best known folded paper art, offers intriguing compositions created from a few carefully-placed folds.

▲ **FOLDED BAG.** The folding instructions (right) prove how easy it is to fold this little bag. The green paper is stamped with a delicate all-over pattern. The silver mizuhiki cord handle and little glass flower clasp are just the right embellishments.

1. Start with a square piece of paper, patterned side down.

2. Fold in half diagonally, and crease.

3. Fold the right lower corner up and across to meet the opposite diagonal edge, creating a straight horizontal line across the base triangle. Crease.

4. Fold the lower left corner of the base triangle up and across to the opposite edge, right along the horizontal line created by the right corner fold. Crease.

5. Round the edge of the top point.

6. Fold down the top point, across the horizontal line created by the two previous folds. Crease.

◄ **PLEATED POCKET.** This little pleated pocket uses the same basic folds, or pleats, as the card, opposite. The turquoise paper is stamped in white pigment ink. The tiny tag, cut from the template included with this book, with its jaunty yellow and white ribbon, tucks into any one of the pleated folds.

◀ **PLEATED CARD** by Patti Behan. The pleated violet column down the left side of this card adds texture and dimension. The flat darker purple ribbon bands the pleats. The elegant monochromatic palette with varying shades of ivory in the patterned background paper, mat, and central panel support the regal purple of the flower, ribbon, and pleated column.

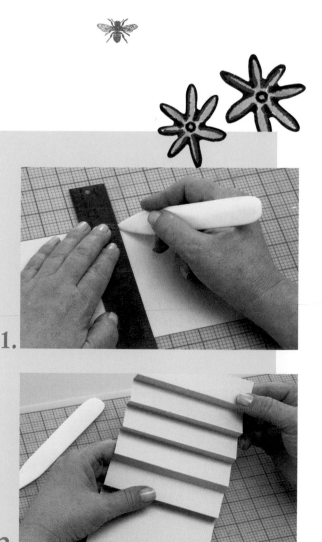

1. Anchor a piece of violet cardstock to a grid-lined cutting board. Using a bone folder and a ruler, score alternately every inch and every half inch across the surface of the cardstock.

2. Make alternate mountain and valley folds on the scored lines (We created mountain folds on the one-inch lines, and valley folds on the one-half-inch lines.).

The final step is to trim the pleated panel to the desired size and attach to a midnight blue mat, and then to the card.

◄▲ **SELF-CLOSING ENVELOPES** by Adrienne Kennedy. Large, square self-closing envelopes in beige and pink patterned papers are a special treat for the recipient. Stamp the tag with a coordinating ink color, and set aside. Create a square card out of cardstock. Stamp and embellish the card, as desired. Place the card like a diamond in the middle of the reverse side of the printed paper, and using the card as a guide, score all four sides. Fold each point of the paper at the scored lines into the center of the card. Add the embellished tag with a velcro dot.

◄◄ **BIRTHDAY PACKAGE** by Kim Smith. Party hats and party horns set the stage for a celebration. Simple white wrapping paper is stamped in several colors and tied with coordinating polka dot ribbon. The accompanying gift card is created using the template on page 128. Two white paper circles and two blue paper circles intertwine over a square to form the card. The same stamps and ribbon embellish the card.

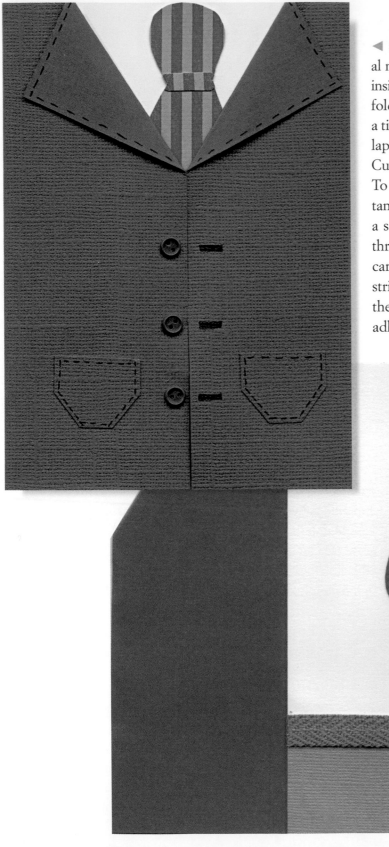

◀ **CARD FOR DAD** by Kim Smith. Surprise Dad with a personal message that appears when you lift the handkerchief from the inside pocket. Start by folding brown cardstock into a gatefold card, folding out the inside corners to form jacket lapels. Freehand cut a tie, handkerchief, message strip, and pockets. Stitch around the lapels and pockets, and create buttonholes using a fine-point pen. Cut inside cardstock to represent the shirt, pocket, and trousers. To create the belt buckle, use a ribbon punch to punch two rectangles in gold cardstock. Then center the two rectangle holes in a square punch and punch out. Run a natural tan twill ribbon through the two holes and around the back. Before assembling the card, cut a slit above the pocket of the shirt and insert the message strip with the handkerchief attached. When attaching the inside of the card to the cover, be sure to keep the message area free of adhesive. Attach buttons to the front of the jacket.

▼ POP-UP CARD. What could be more fun than receiving a card that pops up to wish you a happy birthday? The party cat and balloons are on one stamp. Stamp them in black, color with watercolor, and cut out. Attach strings to each balloon, cut slits on the top and bottom of the cat's paw and insert the ends of the string behind the paw. You will need to construct two pop-up elements. To make the first one, cut two parallel rectangular slits along the inner fold of the card. Score at the top and bottom of the slits, gently pull the pop-up stand forward and attach the cat. To make the second stand, for the balloons, cut a ¹/₂- by 2 ¹/₂-inch strip of cardstock and fold it into five equal parts. Attach the first piece of the strip to the last piece to form a ¹/₂-inch-wide square. Postition this square onto the card and the balloons onto the pop-up box. Layer the card to cover the pop-up. Stamp "Happy Birthday."

you deserve the best!

▲ IRIS FOLD. Iris folding gets its name from the "eye" or iris of the shutter of a camera. Folded papers are arranged in a spiral pattern to create a central opening that appears to have layers of shutters around it. The palette for this charming card is four shades and/or patterns of summer-flower pink cradled in the opening of a punched leafy green tag.

WELCOME TO THE FAMILY by Trish Turay. Start making this four-fold tag by accordion-folding cardstock. After folding, cut the tops into a tag shape. Layer with printed papers, ribbons, punches, stamps, inks, and more tags. The soft muted colors of the preprinted paper provide a wonderful palette for the other papers, inks, and ribbons.

◄ **DREAM** by Kim Smith. Fast to make with great results, this DREAM card is created with Classic Lettering Stencils. Accordion fold the cardstock into five pages. Each page should be the size of the individual letter stencil. Before mounting the stencils on the cardstock, randomly stamp the entire surface. Stipple to add color, using a brush and ink pads. With a gold leafing pen, outline each letter and the outside edge of each stencil. Attach the letters to the folded cardstock.

▲ **FOLDED BOOK-IN-A-BOX** by Laurie Goodson. This elegant stamped, folded book-in-a-box deserves to sit open on a table or desk. Start with square sheets of paper that when folded into four squares equal the size of the inside of the box. Open up the folded square and "squash"-fold two opposite sides. Repeat this for every section in the accordion fold. When putting the sections together, glue one square inside the previous one so the squash-fold sections are on opposite sides. Stamp, write, and stipple to your heart's content, making this an impressive and personal gift for a favorite friend. See the template on page 126.

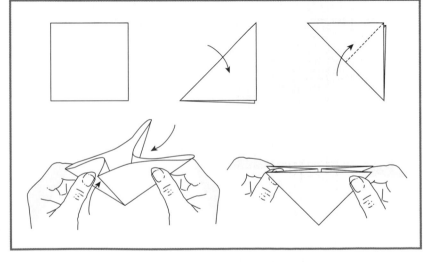

▲ **NOAH, SPRING 2000.** How do you not fall in love with this little cowboy? Smiling at Mom, a wistful break, and winking at the photographer are all in a day's work. Moments like these cannot be forgotten. Basic colors: black and white, silver and red. Photo corner folding instructions are at left.

▶ **DUE IN DECEMBER.** A moment of unmitigated joy before the baby is born. The photograph was a gift for the husband and father-to-be, and now is the first page of the family scrapbook. See page 127 for the folding template for the photo frame.

Due in December

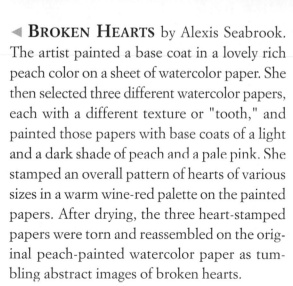

UNDER THE SEA by Alexis Seabrook. Two similar studies in blue, both creating patterns and rhythm with shapes stamped and torn. The two palettes are a contrast in blue-green tones. The lighter image (bottom) offers a pale watery background eliciting the depths of a calm morning sea. The dramatic, darker collage draws us into a more active sea. The artist stamped on a watercolor-wash background, tore the paper when it was dry, and reassembled the pieces onto a watercolor-washed heavy watercolor paper. She stamped again, over the assembled images, with harmonizing highlights.

◀ **BROKEN HEARTS** by Alexis Seabrook. The artist painted a base coat in a lovely rich peach color on a sheet of watercolor paper. She then selected three different watercolor papers, each with a different texture or "tooth," and painted those papers with base coats of a light and a dark shade of peach and a pale pink. She stamped an overall pattern of hearts of various sizes in a warm wine-red palette on the painted papers. After drying, the three heart-stamped papers were torn and reassembled on the original peach-painted watercolor paper as tumbling abstract images of broken hearts.

◄ **STAMPED PAPER QUILT.** A paper quilt literally put together inch-by-inch is filled with light. Collage is often thought of as an assemblage of papers torn in a free form style, but a geometric quilt pattern such as this pretty one might change your mind. This delightful, fresh quilt is made with eight different spring-like color papers, each one stamped with columns of images created with a different background stamp.

1. Cut eight different color cardstock papers into strips slightly wider than the stamps you have selected. Stamp each image in a coordinating ink color down the length of the paper strip.

2. Punch the stamped strips into one-inch squares, turning the punch upside-down so you can center the portion to be punched. Arrange the squares in a diagonal pattern on ivory coverstock, and glue in place. We started at the top left corner of the cardstock. You can use cut pieces of the quilt to create a variety of projects, if you wish.

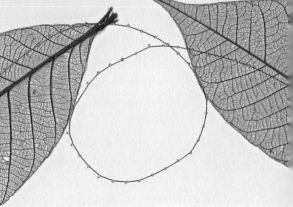

Wishing you
a very happy day

Just Because

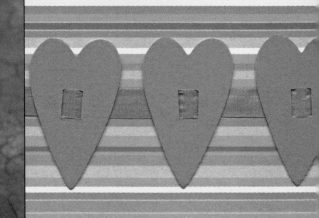

WEAVING, STITCHING & QUILLING

Many of the techniques used by fiber artists are effective with paper projects. Quilting and weaving are two of the most effective techniques adapted by paper crafters. Interlaced strips of complementary or contrasting color, texture, and patterned paper or ribbon create the illusion of rich woven fabrics. The weaving can be the focus of the project or it can be a decorative embellishment.

Paper crafters have discovered the joy of adding stitches sewn with thread to their paper projects. It needn't be difficult. A single line of machine stitching holding a leaf onto a card, is as effective as embellishing ric-rac with embroidery thread of a contrasting color. It is the added texture of the stitching as well as a surprise element that creates interest.

Quilling, also known as paper filigree, is a fascinating dimensional paper craft using thin strips of papers that are wound around a narrow tool. The rolled coils are shaped into interesting decorative designs.

People who are new to paper quilling or paper filigree often mistake it to be a simple "craft" when in reality it is a genuine art form that is more than 500 years old. Once considered an acceptable pastime for European "Ladies of Leisure," museums in Europe today showcase many fine examples of entire pieces of furniture and framed pictures covered entirely with gilded quilling.

With a little bit of curling and pinching we take simple narrow pieces of paper and form them into some of the most beautiful finished images possible.

WEAVING

R epeated images can produce pleasing rhythmic effects. The ribbons weaving in and out of the punched shapes or the woven paper strips have a pleasing rhythm of their own. The textural contrast of punched cardstock and silk ribbon is pleasing. Woven paper produces a richer fabric, resembling the texture of woven tapestry.

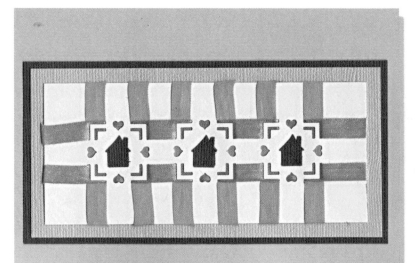

NEW ADDRESS

Creating the project:

◄ **PUNCHED SAMPLER**

1.Punch three copies of a quilt block in a row on ivory card stock. Punch the same shape three times on brown cardstock. Keep the house shapes and toss the remaining border.

2. Weave a narrow pink silk ribbon both horizontally and vertically through each punched block, over the outer rim, under the block, and over the opposite outer rim. See the whole punched block shape in brown below.

3. Tuck the ends of the ribbons behind the punched cardstock before mounting the panel on pink and brown mats. Glue the brown house shapes in place.

4. Finally, attach the brown mat to a light green card.

5. Stamp the message along the bottom of the card.

TIP

For easy alignment of the three images, punch the center image first, followed by the two sides.

◄ **WOVEN MAT.** The woven mat of textured paper adds rhythm and depth to the simple stamped card. The layers of woven papers and mats draw the eye directly to the featured colored dragonfly. You can vary the size of the paper strips.

▶ **PUNCHED HEARTS.** We threaded these five punched pink hearts with purple ribbon by cutting slits in the middle of each heart with a ribbon punch. Weave the ribbon through the slits to anchor the hearts to the patterned paper. Tuck the ribbon behind the striped paper before attaching it to the purple cardstock. Layer the mats onto an ivory card and stamp the message along the bottom of the card. The consistent orientation of all of the elements on this card (hearts, ribbon, striped paper, borders top and bottom—all horizontal) contribute to the ordered feeling generated by it.

greetings

Weaving creates a wonderful effect. You can create cards to feature the weaving as we have with these two, or use the weaving to accent stamped images as we have with the card on the bottom of the opposite page. These woven ribbons are dramatically presented within shaped frames—a flower and an oak leaf—with appropriate color palettes. The process is the same as the two projects opposite, but the effect is very different. The focus is the woven shape.

▼ **WOVEN OAK LEAF AND WOVEN FLOWER.** Start by weaving the ribbons. We like to work with an uneven number of ribbons—three or five different colors. Tape a row containing one each of the ribbons along a horizontal line on cardstock. Then tape a vertical column of the ribbons along the left side of the cardstock. Start weaving the vertical bottom ribbon under and over the horizontal row, leaving the excess loose at the right side (to be tightened and taped down later. Weave the second vertical ribbon under and over across the columns of ribbons. Continue in this manner until you have woven all rows of ribbon. Punch a shape to layer over the woven ribbon pattern.

Just Because

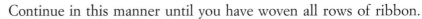

We designed the oak leaf so the green ribbon would only appear at the outer tips of the leaf.

83

STITCHING

🐝

Stitching adds texture, color, and intrigue. Try it! The addition of bright red ric-rac stitched with blue embroidery thread brings a delightful homespun touch to this charming card. The anchor and sailboat shapes punched out of the green cardstock add a jaunty note. The blue stitching on the ric-rac echoes the stitch lines on the overalls. The color palette is simple but effective—denim blue, bright red, and apple green.

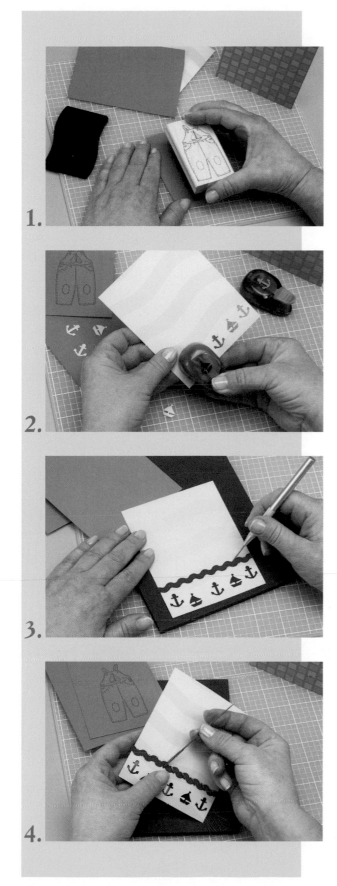

1.

2.

3.

4.

1. Cut two pieces of blue cardstock and one piece of green swirl cardstock to the appropriate size. Trim one piece of the blue cardstock slightly larger than the overalls stamp. Stamp the overalls image onto this cardstock. Color the stamped image with colored pencil and add the two little red buttons. Cut out the stamped overalls.

2. Cut the green swirl cardstock about 1/8 inch all around smaller than the blue piece. Punch the anchor and sailboat shapes out of the green cardstock in an uneven line near the bottom of the green cardstock.

3. Cut a strip of red ric-rac a little wider than the card. Stretch across the green cardstock just above the punched out shapes, and glue it down. Poke small holes in the green cardstock, with an awl, in the valleys of the ric-rac.

4. Stitch over and under the valleys of the ric-rac with blue doubled embroidery thread to create textural contrast. Attach the colored stamped overalls image onto the green cardstock, Center the punched green cardstock onto the blue cardstock and glue it down lightly. Attach these two layers to a blue patterned card, positioned so that there is an equal margin of the blue checks.

TIP
Use colored pencils to add color to dark cardstock. Markers and watercolors will not provide accurate colors.

Remember to collect the positive punched shapes for use with another project.

◄ **DECORATED BOXES.** The box is a cube. We bordered the white birthday box with a dark blue ribbon layered with red ric-rac and crystal stitching, grounding the Happy Birthday message centered in each panel . The simple red-matted birthday cake centered on top of the cube completes the balance. Straightforward lines of varying weights and textures combined with the centered figures contribute to the sense of balance and proportion. The tiny baby-blue box is wrapped at its center in white ric-rac and yellow stitching. The announcement on the diagonal on the top of the cube echoes the angle of the stitching lines.

▶ **HELIUM MAN.** A charming little offbeat figure stands gawkily clutching a pink heart balloon. Pink zig-zag stitching divides the card into two horizontal and two vertical panels. The card is divided in half horizontally by jagged stitching, the figure on the right and a vertical striped paper on the left. The card is also divided vertically with a broad band of pink and white polka dots at the top and a narrow grounding band of brown and white polka dots layered with pink loopy ribbon at the bottom. The horizontal and vertical paper panels recede to give weight to the silly distorted stamped figure who looks like he might follow the balloon at any moment. Our eye knows just where to go.

FLOATING LEAVES. In this simplest of examples, stitching is incorporated on a stamped and embellished card. Autumn colored leaves are attached to a landscape-shape card and their swirling shapes are connected with windblown, swirling red thread stitching. The simple message is stamped in black ink. It's a good thing to remember that not every card has to be an important work of art. Sometimes it is more important just to let people know that you are thinking of them. In this case, perhaps an old friend loves autumn leaves, or loves the song "Autumn Leaves." The red leaves stitched on a card may be enough to remind them of a special moment or time.

"B-A-B-Y". Baby discs with baby letters stamped on pale pink cardstock rimmed in darker pink arc all stitched together across the top. The little ducky pull toy stamped and colored with colored pencil on a pink panel has tiny buttons for wheels. Four small white buttons anchor the four corners of the panel. The purple card provides a dramatic backdrop for the softer color features.

QUILLING

Rubber stamping has long been a hugely enjoyable hobby for many of us. It is easily brought into the crafts of scrapbooking and paper quilling... and a great way to justify an addiction to rubber stamps! "I actually now find I look at stamps from a totally different perspective than ever before. If I can quill it... I buy it!" says Jan Williams, our quilling expert.

BASIC QUILLED SHAPES

LOOSE GLUED COIL

Roll the paper on the quilling tool to form a coil. Remove the coil from the tool. Allow the coil to relax and expand to desired size, and apply small amount of glue to the end of paper strip, gluing down to the coil.

TIGHT COIL

Roll the paper on the quilling tool to form a coil. DO NOT allow the coil to relax and expand. While the coil is still on the tool, apply small amount of glue to the end of paper strip, gluing down to the coil. Gently remove the coil from tool.

TEARDROP

Make a loose glued coil. Pinch at one end of the coil to form a teardrop shape.

SHAPED TEARDROP

Make a teardrop. Run your fingernail toward the point curling the point in one direction.

SQUARE

Make a loose glued coil. Flatten the coil between the fingers. Hold the flattened coil upright between thumb and index finger with the points at the top and bottom. Flatten again matching up the previous 2 folds created by the points. Reopen to form a square shape.

HALF CIRCLE

Make a loose glued coil. Flatten one side of the coil by pinching the circle at two points or flatten coil gently against finger.

Quilling Shapes and Instructions by Jan Williams

BASIC QUILLED SHAPES

TRIANGLE

Make a teardrop shape. Hold the teardrop at the pointed end between the thumb & index finger. Gently press the rounded end back until 3 points are formed.

SHAPED MARQUISE

Make a marquise. Run your fingernail toward one point curling it up. Repeat at the other end curling in the opposite direction.

MARQUISE

Make a loose glued coil. Pinch at the exact opposite side of coil to form points at both ends, forming a marquise shape.

OPEN HEART

Fold a piece of paper in half. Rolling towards the centerfold, roll each end of paper inward toward the centerfold.

RECTANGLE

Make a loose glued coil. Flatten the coil between the fingers. Hold the flattened coil upright between thumb & index finger with points at the top & bottom. Slowly begin to flatten the coil once again moving the previous points slightly away from each other rather than matching them as in the square shape. Reopen to form a rectangle.

BUNNY EAR

Make a loose glued coil. Gently push the coil against the quilling tool (1/4" diameter) to form a shape similar to the crescent, however with the 2 points closer together.

HOLLY LEAF

Make a loose glued coil. Flatten the coil between the fingers. Hold the flattened coil in the center tightly with tweezers. Gently push one end towards center with index finger & thumb forming 2 more points. Repeat on opposite end. Reshape leaf as needed.

ROLLED HEART (ARROW)

Make a teardrop. Hold the teardrop shape between the thumb and index finger of one hand. Gently push the center of rounded end back using the straight edge of the tweezers. Crease at both sides of the pushed-in end.

CRESCENT

Make a teardrop. Pinch one more point not quite opposite of the first point. Run your fingernail toward both points curling the points up or make a loose glued coil. Press coil against the rounded side of the quilling tool or finger to give the coil a crescent shape.

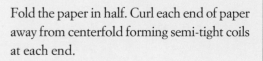

"V" SHAPE

Fold the paper in half. Curl each end of paper away from centerfold forming semi-tight coils at each end.

Quilling Shapes and Instructions by Jan Williams

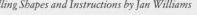

If
friends
were
flowers,
I'd pick
you.

FRIENDLY FLOWERS by Jan Williams. Stamps in two sizes start the garden growing on this soft deckled-edge greeting card. It's almost impossible to imagine this tumble of garden blossoms without the added dimension of the quilled blooms. They fit just right; not too many, and not too few; not too large, and not too small; not too loud, and not too quiet.

ROTATING CARD by Jan Williams. A cool aqua, quilled in the same color swivels against a printed paper in aqua and gold tones. The palette focuses one's attention on the dominant swiveling showpiece.

DUCKS IN A ROW by Jan Williams. The three quilled ducks in a row pop off the page as they reach for the freedom of the card's edge. The dimension of the three quilled ducks is in sharp contrast to the receding background of stamped ducks. The monochromatic palette (with accent exceptions) supports the basic design concept.

▲ **QUILLED RIBBON TAGS** by Jan Williams. Two small quilled yellow rose bouquets drop from rich dark green ribbon ends wrapping a bright green package. The color is strong, and the idea captivating. A stamp provides the base of flowers and leaves. Tiny twirled pieces adds further dimension.

◄ FLORAL NOTE CARDS by Jan Williams. Two flower stamps provided the basis for these delightful stamped and quilled folded note cards or gift tags. Before stamping, the artist spritzed some yellow ink on the cards with a toothbrush. The wonderful loopy stemmed daisy is made with green paper for the leaves and bright yellow and blue petals. For the yellow teardrop petals, make a loose coil and pinch one end. To create the leaves, form a teardrop and bend a pinched end to one side. For the blue-bell, make a loose coil and a shaped crescent.

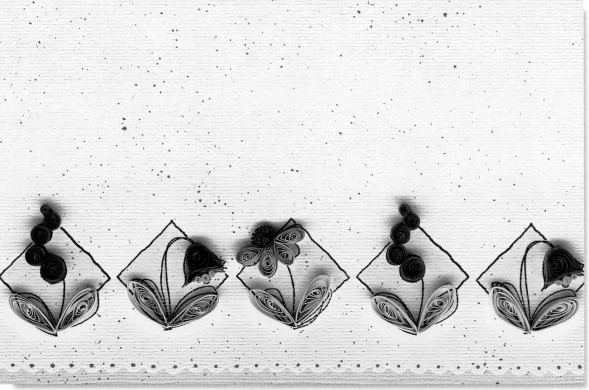

► DANCING FLOWERS by Jan Williams. This card is well prepared before the quilled shapes are added. The card is spritzed with yellow ink and the bottom is trimmed with a decorative edge. The sunny palette is continued with orange dots sitting in the crescents along the decorated edge and a yellow border attached behind the cut edge. The flowers are colorful and rhythmic.

Small, silhouetted tags provide a delightful touch to a small wrapped package.

▶ **QUILLED GOOSE EGG** by Jan Williams. This stunning sculptural piece offers an over-all pattern stamped on a painted goose egg embossed in gold and then embellished with quilled ivory blooms.

▼ **QUILLED JAR AND CANDLE** by Jan Willliams. Using the already designed stamped images provides not only a great pattern for the quilled shapes but also adds to the presentation of the finished work. Stamp the image, color it in, and highlight with coordinating quilled embellishments. The end result will captivate anyone and put many more miles on those rubber stamps!

▶ **LOVE** Jan Williams. An old-fashioned romantic palette. Stamped in an old rose tint, and quilled in delicate pinks and the softest greens, the lovely palette takes us back to the turn of the twentieth century, when times were gentler and there was time for such romance.

QUILLING ROSES

1. Hold the quilling tool perpendicular in the right hand. Thread the quilling paper onto tool from the left, with the paper horizontal to the tool. Roll the paper towards the left until you have made 1½ complete turns around the tool.

3. Start with a square of paper. Making the rest of your folds: Repeat the same instructions used for the first fold until you are at the end of your paper strip. Generally 3 inches of paper will yield 7-9 folds.

Quilling Shapes and Instructions by Jan Williams

2. With the left hand, fold the paper down towards your body. The quilling paper should now be perpendicular against the tool, both going in the same direction. Hold the paper firmly in the left hand and rotate your right arm up while holding the tool to make the paper form a cone shape on the end of the tool. Bring your right arm back down keeping the "cone" shape.

4. Remove the folded rose from the tool. Hold the center of the rose with pointed tweezers and gently turn the paper outward, the opposite way you originally folded the paper. Gently fold the petals down by grabbing several layers of folds with the tweezers and pulling them down away from the center of the rose. Gently "smash" the rose between two fingers before gluing it in place.

▲ **CRIMPED FLOWER** Jan Williams. The vertically-divided background provides the impetus for the color division of the flower. Playing with the color this way adds a wonderful creative dimension to the card. The quilled bloom is made from crimped paper—another quirky creative step contributing to the stunning effect.

▲ **FLOATING BLOSSOM** Jan Williams. The artist quilled the bloom inside the outline shape of the stamped flower. The shape and a palette as softly romantic as our great-grandmothers. The texture of the quilled bloom and the crimped leaves are enticing. It's almost impossible to resist touching.

EMBELLISHING

Who of us has not embellished a story, spiced it up a bit, when we felt it was flat or not interesting enough? Card makers and scrapbookers do the same thing. They embellish their pages with decorative accents to "lift them up," to add style and visual interest.

Recently there has been an explosion in the materials available for crafters to decorate their work. There is an exciting assortment of fibers, metallic pieces, special paper products, and buttons and bows that can turn your one-dimensional projects into three-dimensional creative wonders.

Explore the design possibilities and the inspiring array of stunning embellishments with us. Paper crafters love to adapt techniques and materials from other crafts. We see cards and scrapbook pages that are layered with various colors and size mats, die cuts, tags, fasteners; paper that is folded, torn, cut, punched, quilled, woven, and pierced; buttons, beads, sequins and jewels; stickers, three-dimensional foam tape or dots to lift items off the page; metallic brads or eyelets, or charms; ribbons, yarn, thread to name a few! And the list keeps growing.

We are all storytellers, and those stories can be told verbally, through the written word, or even through our crafted projects. We need to see as well as hear the stories.

Think outside the box. If something appeals to you, try it! Follow your instinct. You'll have fun, and that, after all, is what crafting is all about.

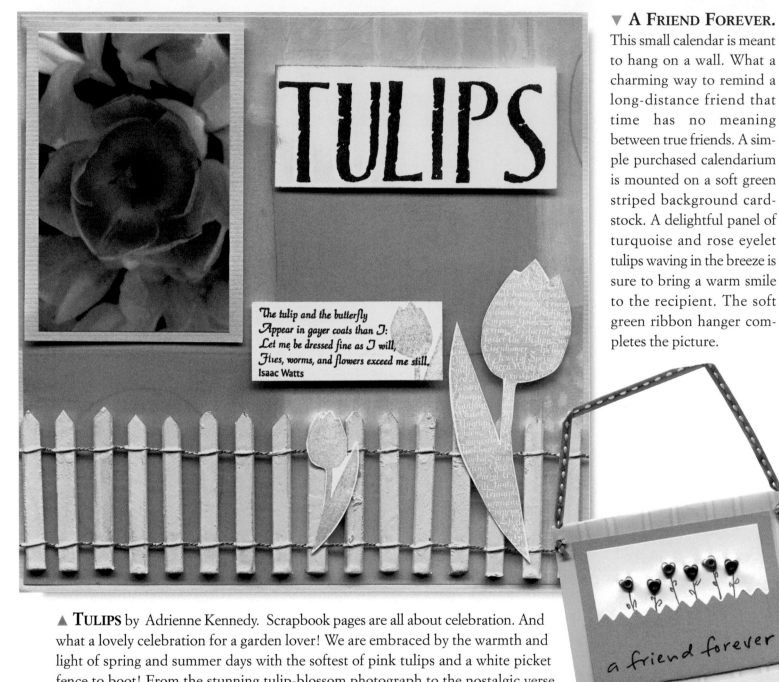

This small calendar is meant to hang on a wall. What a charming way to remind a long-distance friend that time has no meaning between true friends. A simple purchased calendarium is mounted on a soft green striped background cardstock. A delightful panel of turquoise and rose eyelet tulips waving in the breeze is sure to bring a warm smile to the recipient. The soft green ribbon hanger completes the picture.

The tulip and the butterfly
Appear in gayer coats than I:
Let me be dressed fine as I will,
Flies, worms, and flowers exceed me still.
Isaac Watts

▲ **TULIPS** by Adrienne Kennedy. Scrapbook pages are all about celebration. And what a lovely celebration for a garden lover! We are embraced by the warmth and light of spring and summer days with the softest of pink tulips and a white picket fence to boot! From the stunning tulip-blossom photograph to the nostalgic verse printed on simple cardstock to the subtle pastel background palette we are brought along to a perfect day. The three-dimensional white picket fence grounds the colorful photograph and strong title type. The soft pink tulips floating dreamily off the page were stamped and silhouetted.

HEARTFELT THANKS. Here is a novel way to say "thank you"—a tiny glass vial filled with tiny punched pink hearts tied onto a card with blue "eyelash" ribbon. You couldn't say "Thank you with all my heart" in a more delightful way. The focal point is the vial of hearts; and the "thank you," positioned immediately above and below the vial is unavoidable—you can't miss it. The card is easy to make: the background "thank you" and hearts (one stamp) is stamped on cream cardstock, trimmed and layered on a dark mat and green striped paper before being mounted on the card.. The point is clever and well made. If you just remember to keep your eyes open and to have fun, there are inestimable decorative elements and ways to add them to a scrapbook page or a card. This is a keeper!

◀ **OPEN FLOWER.** The flower as a metaphor for life and love; here it is gracefully looped in pink wire and attached at the center to a cheerful geometric stamped background of pink and green diamonds on tan cardstock. The color palette is pleasant and consistent; the design straightforward; the embellishments clean and simple—pink wire, and green and white gingham ribbon tied jauntily across the bottom. It all adds up to a warm, clean presentation.

◄ EMBOSSED HEARTS by Annette Watkins. Torn vellum, torn cardstock, several layers of soft colors all tied together dramatically. The central heart is stamped, embossed, and colored; the surrounding one is stamped in white and embossed. Embossing underlines the thought and adds depth to the design without distracting from it. A layer of vellum cardstock adds a bit of intrigue to the pleasing soft and refreshing palette. The ribbons are tied with a swagger at the top with an interesting touch—they poke through holes punched in a cuff of the layered cardstock.

◄▼ A POSY OF VIOLETS by Annette Watkins. Gentle colors for gentle thoughts. A bouquet of stamped and watercolored violets is the focal point of this charming card decorated with bows, a bead, eyelets, and even a tag peeking out from behind the scene, complete with a curly cord. Many layers of materials all coordinated, offering many layers of intention?

i love you

◄ A QUIET NOTE. Beautiful silk knots anchor the four corners of a decorative-edged mat. Simple layering of pleasing colors is the perfect setting. But centerstage belongs to a quiet violet stamped envelope (made with one of our templates) out of which a tiny tag is lifted. Lovely accoutrements for a lovely message; something one could tuck in a pocket or bag to carry throughout the day. A simple "I love you"—you don't need much more.

▲ **ROSE** by Adrienne Kennedy. Rose, the flower of love, tells all here. A soft, subtle palette lets the photograph present the story. The added "bells and whistles" shout the message to all—metallic-rimmed tags, die-cut roses, a meaningful quote, coordinated ribbons, a half-hidden butterfly charm, and a touching photograph. There are a lot of elements on this page—more than most. If the colors were loud, the page would not work. It is the quiet palette that lets the many layers of additional elements contribute to the page, rather than detract from it. It's something like building a sandcastle one drip at a time.

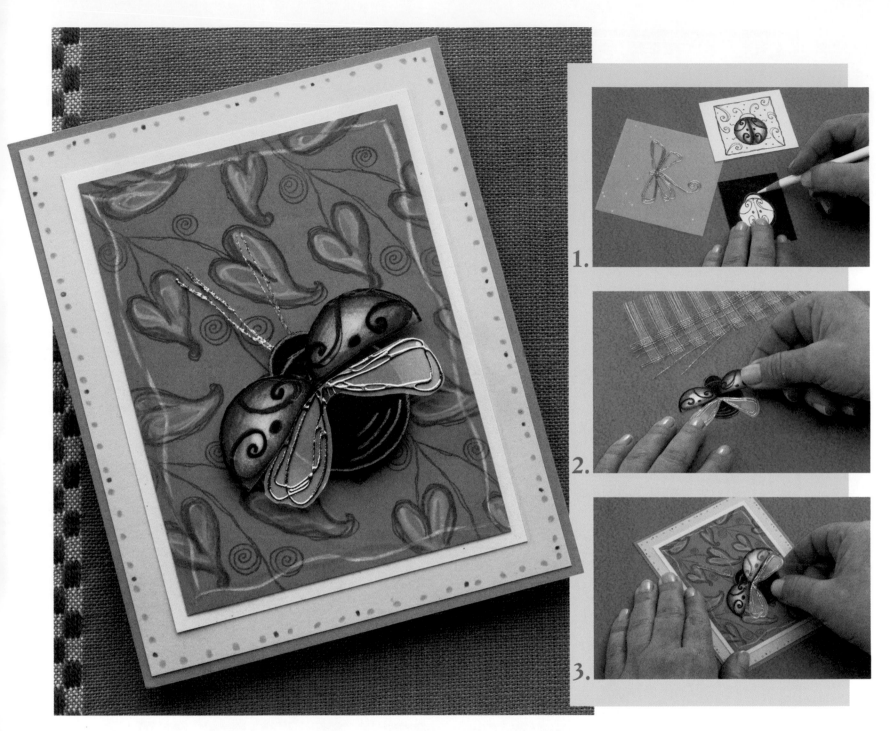

▲ **FLYING LADYBUG** by Marie-Eve Trudeau. This lady-bug is on the move. Here she is, poised above a garden of hearts, ready to take flight at will. Now in a somewhat altered state, she started out as a one-piece bug with a circle body. This is a good example of letting your imagination take hold, playing with the materials, and having fun with your stamps. This designer cut a rather static stamped image apart and added the parts to another stamped image. We could call this an amalgam of bugs. The palette is subtle and effective. The ladybug is the focal point, hovering over the background garden.

1. Stamp the image twice on ivory cardstock. Color the body only of one of the stamped images. Paint it with a clear dimensional lacquer and let it dry. Silhouette the second ladybug (cut out the body only, without the antennae).

2. Use the silhouetted ladybug as a template to draw another ladybug in white pencil on black cardstock. Add a white pencil border around the shape, and add highlights at the base of the body. Cut this one out.

Cut the colored ladybug in half vertically. Mount the halves like wings on each side of the black body. Add a second pair of wings cut from a Peel-Off's dragonfly mounted on vellum and cut to take only the wings.

3. Stamp brown cardstock with brown ink and enhance with colored pencil. Draw a freehand frame around with colored pencils around the edge of the stamped cardstock, and color the edges of the cardstock with green ink. Layer the stamped cardstock on ivory, chamois, and pumpkin cardstocks. The chamois is enhanced with dots made with colored pencils.

Add gold antennae to the ladybug with a few gold threads cut from maruyama paper. Add the sculpted ladybug to the stamped cardstock layered with coordinating mats. Attach the ladybug with mounting tape to raise the image off the paper.

▲ **BALLERINA DRESS** by Kim Smith. The graceful ballerina bodice is enhanced with a delicate skirt of sheer silk organza ribbon tucked into a slit at the dropped waistline. The image is stamped in brown and enhanced with colored pencils. The flowers are tinted with a rose-colored pencil. Both the dress neckline and the flower centers are finished with a clear glitter gel pen.

◄ **CROSSWORD LOVER** by Kim Smith. The perfect card for the crossword-puzzle lover in your family. This is so simple to construct. Believe it or not, the crossword puzzle is a stamp!

Creating the Project:

1. Stamp the crossword puzzle in black ink on white cardstock.

2. Add the small H-A-P-P-Y B-I-R-T-H-D-A-Y beads in your own pattern.

3. Layer the stamped crossword off the edge of a slightly smaller mat of black cardstock, so that part of the mat is visible at the top and left side of the stamped image.

4. Mount the layered crossword image onto a red card.

5. Make a slit in the fold of the card, near the bottom edge. (This one is about an inch up from the bottom.) Tie a black and white gingham ribbon around the card front, tucking it through the slit.

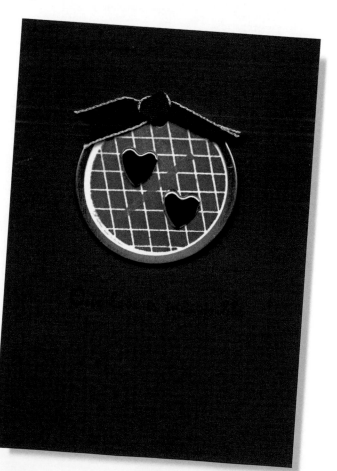

► **A SIMPLE VALENTINE.** One simple stamped line and one simple decorated tag. The design and the color of this card could not be simpler. But the placement is strong, and the simplicity adds to the power. Less is often more. A metal-rimmed tag embraces two small metal hearts and a dividing line on a red-and-white plaid background. The ribbon ties it together. Nothing will divide these hearts: A simple and clever execution of a meaningful thought.

TIP

Save unused bits of ribbon for future use. It's a real treat to dig into a box or bag of ribbon remnants to add to your projects.

▼ **LOVE.** Each letter squarely in its own red tag bedecked with red and white gingham ribbon, hangs from the stars against a stark black background. The charming lowercase letters made with our alphabet, have their own whimsy. The simple design of the staggered line of letters has wonderful rhythm and energy.

▲ **RIBBONS FROM HEAVEN.** The texture of ribbons can be so sumptuous and appealing that sometimes you need very little more to create a beautiful card. These grosgrain ribbons—three warm colors—harmonize and are tied together by the repetitive white polka dots. Warm colors for warm thoughts.

Three ribbons are wrapped around white cardstock and attached at the back with tape. The knots tied at the ends of the other three ribbons are held in place with glue dots. The stamped Happy Birthday message is layered on an orange mat and then onto the card, right over the ribbons. The beribboned white card is mounted onto brown cardstock.

▼ **DRAGONFLIES IN FLIGHT,** by Dave Brethauer. Three fluttering dragonflies in a column look like they could head off the top of the card in formation, creating a strong sense of motion. The dragonflies are stamped in black, colored with pencils, and finished with dimensional glitter.

▲ **BLUE MAGIC** by Nathalie Métivier. One rubber stamp and silver Peel-Off's were used to create this stunning card. The stamping is really simple, but the assembling makes it shine The rubber stamp for this frame-within-a-frame card is one large stamp. Be sure to press with a strong even touch on such a large stamp. The outer margin is created with silver Peel-Off's.

Creating the project:
1. Stamp the center image with Iris Blue Fluid chalk on light blue cardstock. Cut it out leaving a $1/16$th-inch border around the first frame. Mount on steel blue cardstock.
2. On a larger piece of light blue cardstock, create a frame using silver Peel-Off's. Layer on two blue cardstocks—steel blue and dark blue.
3. Decorate the four corners of a small dark blue cardstock square with the same silver Peel-Off's leaves you used to decorate the outer frame. Mount in the center of the silver Peel-Off's frame.
4. Turn the center panel square to a diamond shape (rotate 90 degrees clockwise) and layer onto the small dark blue square.
5. Add three strands of maruyama silver threads held together with tiny Peel-Off's circles to the top and bottom edges of the large dark blue card. Mount this onto dark blue cardstock. You now have a frame on a frame. Decorate the interior triangles with Peel-Off's silver leaves.

▶ **CHRISTMAS STAMPS** by Marie-France Perron. A fantasy of hand-colored Christmas stamps float on a vellum cloud, celebrating the peace of the season. The palette is cool and wintery, a midnight clear.

1.

2.

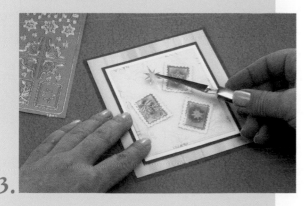

3.

1. Mount three Peel-Off's stamps on white cardstock. Add color —green, turquoise, and purple—with a watercolor pen or a small brush and watercolor paint. Cut the stamped images to postage-stamp size with decorative-edged scissors.

2. Stamp holly pieces on light blue cardstock with smoke blue ink. Layer the blue cardstock on white, blue, and then green paper.

3. Mount the colored stamps on a sheet of vellum paper and cut to fit just inside the edge of the stamped light blue cardstock. Add silver stars. Finish with a border of small silver Peel-Off's stars around the rim of the dark blue cardstock mat.

TIP

Peel-Off's are easily repositionable on cardstock. You can move them around until you find the right composition.

1.

2.

3.

4.

▲ **SUMMER GARDEN** by Nathalie Métivier. The flower is blooming and the butterfly is flying, in this lyrical garden, each of them almost off the page. The stage is set for literally boosting the joys of a summer's day. The stamped- and-colored flower is lifted off the page on a small tile, and the butterfly is poised at the top of a circuitous path. The energy and rhythm are infectious.

1. Stamp the flower with dark green fluid chalk on soft green paper, and enhance with colored pencil. Cover a two-inch square of cardboard with rose patterned paper. Mount the square on it, then on a torn piece of stucco green paper.

2. Color the edge of a large tag, direct-to-paper with a green Cats Eye ink pad. Stamp the oblong flower stamp several times over the tag in dark green ink.

3. Mount the stamped-and-colored flower from Step 1 onto the rose square and attach it to the tag. Mount the tag onto the stucco green and ivory card. Add some gold maruyama threads to make a bow at the top of the tags..

4. Add a Peel-Off's butterfly enhanced with colored pencil and cut. Attach the butterfly to the card with mounting tape to lift it off the surface of the card. Hang a purple wire swirled with some beads below the butterfly.

Finish the card with a Peel-Off's gold border and dots.

TIP

Threads and fibers, and yarns and ribbons can all be tied onto a completed project. And remember that they can be replaced when they begin to look tired. A refreshing bouquet of new fibers, when needed, will keep this charming bookmark in use forever.

▶ **JUST FOR YOU** by Stacey Turechek. A message for any time of the year is brought with this delightful bookmark presentation. A single flower stamped on white cardstock is enhanced with little dots of color and layered on salmon and moss green mats before layering onto pale green stamped cardstock. Green ric-rac, held on with yellow mini brads, wraps around the pale green cardstock. The wrapped card is then mounted on a salmon-colored base. The threads of a carefree fiber bouquet, with colors picked up from the inks and papers below, dance across the top of the card. The palette is sunny and warm, warm enough to warm you up on a winter's day

ABOVE AND BEYOND

What does it mean—above and beyond? Above and beyond what? Well, most of us think of greeting cards or scrapbook pages when considering projects to make with rubber stamps, but unique ideas for rubber stamping abound.

In this chapter we have gathered together some unusual, unexpected projects. We include a rubber-stamped book bound with a shutter latch, a fabulous old-fashioned concertina, a memory book made from lunch bags and bound with ribbons, and a collaged wine box. In some cases, the project involved intricate folding or construction. In others, an everyday object has been transformed into something beautiful. And then, two artists responded to a challenge to create something with a material with which they didn't usually work.

The result? From one, stunning wrapping paper, gift cards, and coordinated ribbon that you would not want to give away. From another, lovely pieces from her journal/sketchbook from a trip to Italy, incorporating rubber stamps with her painted, journaled pages.

We responded immediately to the artists who kept using the word "play" in their descriptions of what they had done. They talked about playing with colors and shapes and textures. And that was the "A-ha" moment. It *is* about play. And it is about being open to new venues. We aren't just rubber stampers or scrapbookers or quillers or watercolorists. We are crafters and artists who are unafraid to use a variety of materials. And we have fun.

BEE BOOK by Laurie Goodson. This intriguing small book uses a few rubber stamps (mostly bees, plus an alphabet) and a few embellishments, including tags and eyelets, and an ingenious spine for the book—a black metal shutter latch. The low-key, supporting palette of varying shades of beige, warm yellow, and brown sets the stage for the featured black metal latch.

▼ **THE MAGIC OF ORDINARY LIFE** by Trish Turay. A playful cover using printed paper in soft colors plus stamped letters in mixed colors, fonts, and cases is tied with jaunty ribbons. The book holds photos and notes on family favorites—favorite corners of the house, favorite recipes.

▶**STAR BOOK** by Laurie Goodson. This old-fashioned, handmade, folded star book opens in a circular motion and is tied with a soft ribbon to form a circle. The palette of autumnal colors, and the grape stamps are pleasing. The multi-layered book binding using harmonious-colored papers is intriguing. We love the intricate star-shapes of the binding.

▲ **FAMILY VACATION.** An ingenious album of a special family vacation is full of tabs and tags to push and pull, and extra layers to unfold. This delightful spread with multiple-stamped topiary images standing sentinel at the bottom of the pages mimic the photographs of the whimsical topiaries.

◄ **WINE BOX COLLAGE.** by Laurie Goodson. The smooth wood of the wine box provides a smooth surface on which to stamp and embellish. Torn paper, metal bits, alphabet tiles, images stamped in black on a warm honey-toned base all contribute to the appealing finish.

► **MOTHER'S DAY BOOK.** by Trish Turay. Earth-toned backgrounds, a gaudy fuschia flower, and lots of ribbons adorn this imaginative book made with lunch bags. Embellishments "to the nines"!

Mom, I will always love you, but I will never forgive you for cleaning my face off with your spit

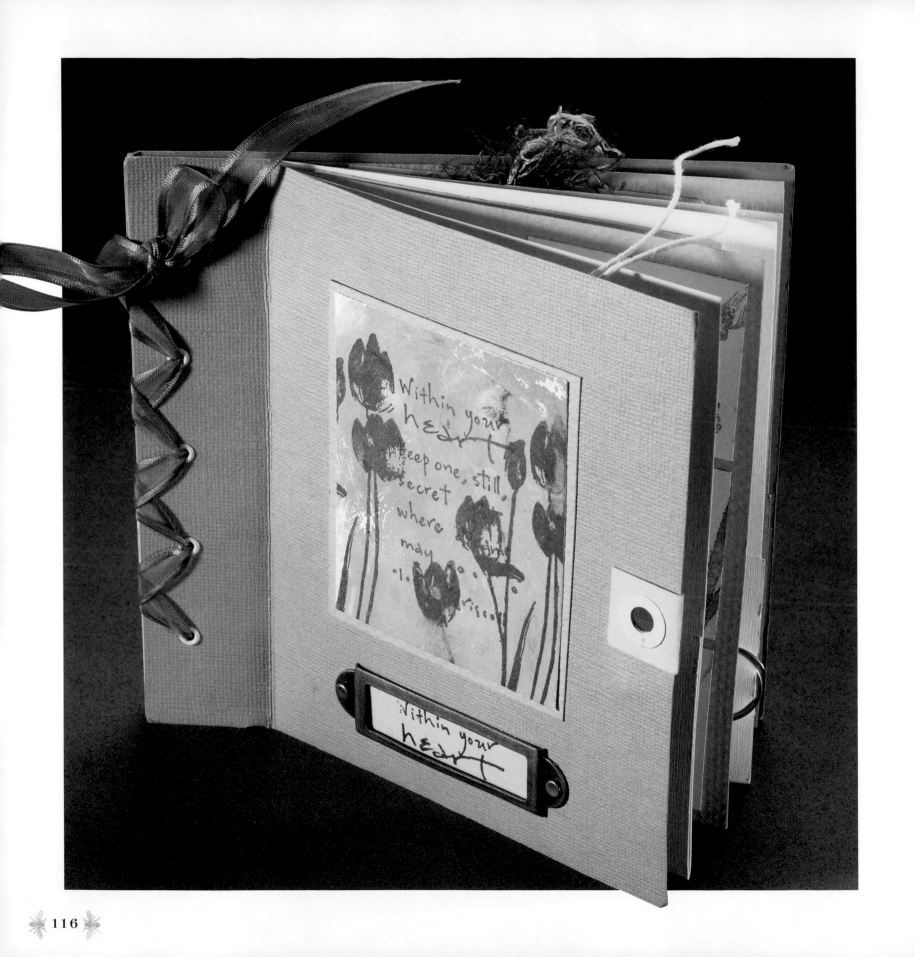

◄▲ **WITHIN YOUR HEART** by Laurie Goodson. A refreshing handmade book is bound with a swirl of silk ribbon. The soft-violet coverstock provides a pleasing platform for the center stamped image of flowers and elegant old handwriting. The metal nameplate frame and office stationery bits add a note of realism to the imaginative package.

The interior of the book is a series of pocket pages, this one filled with tags stamped in bright colors on coordinating background colors. The tags are ready to leap out of the minimally-stamped pocket decorated with a circle clip and micro decorated tag on one side and a brad on the opposite side. We see hints of other treasures in pockets-to-come bright-colored silky yarn reaches out from a back page.

◀▼ **STAMPED GIFT PAPER** by Christine Timmons. Dramatic, sophisticated giftwrap gives gift-giving a whole new dimension—who could give it away? The artist played with stamps of simple shapes accented with occasional surprises. The stamps for the matte-finish magenta paper include copper and aqua ink pads, a few geometric stamps, and a magical silver pen. The surprise element with the brown kraft paper is the block of white lines created with a dinner fork. The black paper is covered with a repetitive arrangement of same-size circles imaginatively embellished.